COMMUNITY CARE PRACTICE HA**N**

General Editor: Martin Davi**c**

The Social Work
and the Courts

COMMUNITY CARE PRACTICE HANDBOOKS

General Editor: Martin Davies

The Social Worker and the Courts

David Wright

HEINEMANN EDUCATIONAL BOOKS
LONDON

Heinemann Educational Books Ltd
22 Bedford Square, London WC1B 3HH

LONDON EDINBURGH MELBOURNE AUCKLAND
HONG KONG SINGAPORE KUALA LUMPUR NEW DELHI
IBADAN NAIROBI JOHANNESBURG
EXETER (NH) KINGSTON PORT OF SPAIN

ISBN 0 435 82977 7

Typeset by The Castlefield Press of High Wycombe
in 10/12 pt Press Roman, and printed in Great Britain by
Spottiswoode Ballantyne Press, Colchester, Essex CO2 8JJ

Contents

Acknowledgements

I wish to express thanks to my publishers for the help and support given to me from the time of acceptance of my manuscript through to publication. I also wish to thank the following for permission to reproduce copyright material on the pages indicated:

Butterworths for the extract from C.C.H. Moriarty, *Police Law* (p. 13) and J.D. McLean, *The Legal Context of Social Work* (p. 2).

The Controller, Her Majesty's Stationery Office, for extracts from: Part 1 of the Children and Young Persons Act 1969 (p. 22), DHSS Health Circulars 76 (20) (p. 58) and 75 (21) (p. 69), and *The Sentence of the Court* (p. 85).

The Editor, *The Magistrate*, for the extract from the issue of March 1973 (p. 45).

David Wright,
July 1979

1. The Social Worker Has a Part to Play

The primary purpose of this short manual is to offer practical guidance to the local authority social worker in relation to his work in the courts, particularly the Juvenile Court, and to examine the roles he may be called upon to play in the court setting.

There are several reasons why guidance of this sort is important. Firstly, there is a growing volume of legislation which affects the social worker in a setting which to many is both unfamiliar and threatening.

It would appear that the days are over when the social work of the courts (with the exception of the Juvenile Court) was the virtual prerogative of the probation service; nowadays the social worker must play a much more prominent part in the adult court scene.

The Children Act 1975 (consolidated by the Domestic Proceedings and Magistrates' Courts Act 1978) has made provision for the transfer of adoption proceedings from the Juvenile to the Domestic Court. It has also introduced a new concept in child legislation, namely custodianship, and hearings in relation to this are also to be dealt with by the Domestic Court.

These provisions affect both the social worker and the probation officer, especially the former, who has a deeper involvement in adoption and custodianship proceedings. (This will be obvious in the study of custodianship orders in Chapter 7 and the duties of guardian *ad litem* in Chapter 8.)

Adoption hearings are not new to the social worker involved in this area, but the setting of a Domestic Court may be much less familiar. The court itself is to be changed, and no Justice may be qualified to sit in a Domestic Court unless he is a member of a Domestic Court Panel, which is a panel of Justices specially selected to deal with domestic proceedings.[1]

The reorganised Domestic Courts have jurisdiction over a wide range of domestic proceedings (see section 79 of the 1978 Act quoted for a full list) including adoption, custodianship, guardianship and matrimonial matters, and it is reasonable to assume that the role of the social worker is likely to be expanded to take in other appropriate proceedings within the Justices' jurisdiction. (In this connection guardianship and matrimonial proceedings are outlined in Chapter 7.)

A second reason for the necessity of this kind of guidance is the importance of social enquiry reports and recommendations in both criminal and civil court proceedings. Many lawyers and others hold the view that social workers have little experience in sentencing, and little knowledge of the courts or penal institutions, but they still feel free to make recommendations relating to these matters.

It has to be admitted that too many workers are pitchforked into court proceedings with insufficient preparation and training for what is or should be a skilled undertaking. A sound grounding in the preparation and presentation of social enquiry reports both in the Juvenile and the Magistrates' Courts is absolutely essential, if either social worker or probation officer is to be effective in court and gain the confidence and respect of others, especially the magistrates with whom the final decision rests. The same applies to welfare reports in guardianship, custodianship and matrimonial proceedings.

Therefore, this manual attempts to offer guidance on the purpose, collation and preparation of reports requested by the court. Chapter 6 covers reports in criminal and care proceedings as they apply to the Magistrates' Court and the Juvenile Court, and Chapter 7 covers those which are prepared for the Domestic Court, with brief comments on those applicable in the County Court and High Court.

The third reason for this book's existence is the author's awareness of the heavy criticism often levelled at the social worker's attitude to the courts. Often this attitude is governed by his unfamiliarity with the court, its aims and purpose. In his book *The Legal Context of Social Work* J.D. McLean has this to say:

> There are some social workers who have distinctly negative attitudes towards courts of law. It may be useful to begin by identifying some of the underlying reasons.
> One basic reason is unfamiliarity with and dislike for the intimidating mumbo jumbo of the courts, or, as the lawyer might prefer to phrase it, the elegant refinements of legal procedure . . .
> At a deeper level, the court may symbolise for some social workers the restricting and dehumanising features they see in the law itself.
> Or in some contexts, a court hearing is a symbol of failure, where casework has failed to remedy an unhappy situation.
> Perhaps the major reason is that the court is the setting for potential conflict between the social worker and those who do not necessarily share his values or seek to advance the same interests.[2]

Certainly there are some social workers whose attitudes towards courts of law are not simply negative but positively condemnatory. In some cases the court is seen as nothing more than a stumbling block to their professional dealings with those in trouble. It may equally be said of course, that the attitude adopted by the bench on occasion is not calculated to change the views of such workers.

The potential conflict between the social worker and the magistrates is thus aggravated, and will continue to persist until they learn to communicate at a much deeper level. The law itself, particularly in the Children and Young Persons Act 1969, exhorts both to develop a good line of communication in the interests of the offender. As we shall see in the following chapters, many statutes pave the way for a good relationship to be established, offering the social worker and probation officer opportunities to assist the court in the proper disposal of a case, and encouraging the court to seek this assistance through the channel of specific requests.

It has to be recognised that the social worker is neither legally trained nor legally minded, although in the field of child care and probation particularly his work is bounded by statute. The magistrate, on the other hand, need not necessarily be legally trained but he must be legally minded. He can pass no judgement nor make any order or sentence outside the concept of the law. Where he has any doubts on matters of law, practice or procedure, he must consult his clerk for advice.

This difference in approach can lead to a situation where the social worker feels threatened and angry — as, for instance, when his professional acumen has guided him towards a certain course of action and the court, interpreting a statute, has halted his progress. This may create the feeling that it is futile to try to help the court, and that attendance at court is unnecessary except to battle against the incompetence of the magistrates.

Failure to attend court, especially for the presentation of reports, is one of the grievances Justices most often have against some social workers. While there may be sound reasons for non-attendance in court, it must be admitted there is often justification for the grievance. There may be some ambiguities in a report which cannot be clarified without the attendance of the social worker or probation officer. If a case has to be adjourned as a result of this it is the defendant who suffers. Also, of course, the social worker's absence deprives the defendant of support at the time of his greatest need.

Many Local Authority Social Services Departments employ a court officer or team of court officers, who perform a considerable volume of work for the department. These officers are most useful, coping with the various court situations which arise, and occasionally bearing the brunt of criticisms meant for their social worker colleagues.

They understand the purpose and requirements of the court, know how proceedings are conducted and all that is involved in any particular case. They are able in many instances to establish a good link between the court and the Local Authority and smooth over difficult situations.

Unfortunately they cannot deal with all persons appearing before the Justices, and at some time or other the individual social worker has to encounter the court situation. To do so with any degree of competence requires knowledge of all that is involved. Although this knowledge and expertise may be available within the social services department it is of no great value to the individual worker unless it is properly disseminated. The worker must learn about the jurisdiction, function and powers of the court and the relevant statutory instruments which link him with the court.

Of particular importance is his need to gain a sounder knowledge of the working of the court. In the first four chapters of this book we shall look at the roles of the magistrate, the Justices' Clerk, the prosecutor and advocate for the defence in criminal proceedings, including the chief witness, the applicant and respondent in civil proceedings and the police.

Emphasis is laid on the study of Chapter 3, which covers the roles of prosecutor, advocate, etc., as these may have to be played by the social worker or probation officer.

The duties of the local authority social worker and the probation officer are sometimes similar, often complementary to each other, and at times quite different. They do not approach their work from identical 'frames of reference' but they frequently employ the same methods to achieve their objectives.

In the broadest terms it could be said that the probation officer is the professional social worker for the court, and the local authority social worker the professional social worker for the community. They have a meeting point within the court setting.

It is appreciated that there is currently considerable discussion and debate about the respective merits of the Juvenile Courts system and other non-adversarial systems practised elsewhere, but comment on this has been purposely avoided. The object of this manual is to provide a practical guide to social workers and probation officers on the part they have to play under existing legislation. Changes may be necessary, and may be effected in the system eventually, or a new system may replace the present one, but until this happens all workers are under an obligation to carry out the present statutes. Disagreement with the system may be sound grounds for making some effort to improve or alter it, but not for ignoring or failing to comply with its requirements. To do so can only work against the defendant.

2. The Magistrate and the Clerk

For the social worker to appreciate his role, or variety of roles in court, he must have some understanding of the roles of others in the court setting. Most court proceedings are essentially a contest between two parties, governed by rules.

The rules differ according to the type of proceedings; for example, care and criminal proceedings in the Juvenile Court are regulated by the Magistrates' Courts (Children and Young Persons) Rules 1970 as amended by the Magistrates' Courts (Children and Young Persons) (Amendment) Rules 1976. Adoption proceedings are governed by the Adoption (High Court) Rules 1976, the Adoption (County Court) Rules 1976 and the Magistrates' Courts (Adoption) Rules 1976.

The magistrate

In the lower courts, that is, the Magistrates' Court and the Juvenile Court, the magistrates, or Justices of the Peace, to give them their official title, must come first among all who take part in court proceedings. They constitute the court, control the scene, decide the issues and make the orders.

The title evolved with the Justices of the Peace Act 1361, but then the appointment to be a Justice was limited to lords and three or four of the most worthy in a county,[1] and the scope of the office was far more extensive than it is today.

As in 1361, Justices of the Peace are appointed in every county in England, extended to include Wales, but their numbers greatly exceed those permitted under the early Act. Although lords may still be counted among their number they are now chosen from all social classes within the community. The Lord Chancellor (The Rt Hon. Lord Elwyn Jones) has said that Justices are appointed 'not only to administer the law but to be a continual reminder to our people that the laws are their laws and not merely the laws of lawyers; and it is they, the public, who administer them through their representatives on the bench.' Before any Justice can take his place on the bench, he has to take the Oath of Allegiance to the reigning monarch and the Judicial Oath. These oaths govern the actions and conduct of the magistracy.

The Juvenile Court

Only Justices who have been appointed to a Juvenile Court Panel can serve on the Juvenile Court. This court, first established in 1908 as a result of the Children Act 1908, is a Court of Summary Jurisdiction, designated a Petty Sessional Court which requires the presence of two or more Justices.[2] The greatest number permitted to sit in a Juvenile Court is three,[3] and though this is the number which normally constitutes the court, proceedings may be heard by two Justices. Exceptionally, as when the adjournment of a case is considered inexpedient, a stipendiary magistrate (who is paid and is generally a barrister or solicitor of some years standing) can sit alone[4] (see page 7).

Additionally, the court must include a man and a woman save in exceptional circumstances,[5] and this is said to be accepted on the analogy that it requires a parent of either sex to bring up a child properly. (This analogy may be challenged, particularly by the good one-parent family. Nevertheless, there is much to be said for having a member of either sex adjudicating in matters pertaining to children.)

Subject to certain provisions, the Justices have jurisdiction to deal with both criminal and civil proceedings, where any offence (other than homicide) or complaint takes place within their Petty Sessional Division. Civil matters are mainly care proceedings and adoption. Criminal proceedings are normally instituted by way of a charge, summons, or warrant, whereas civil proceedings such as care proceedings and adoption are brought by way of complaint or application to the court. A summons or warrant may be issued to ensure the attendance of a respondent in care proceedings, the child involved being a respondent.

Hearings in a Juvenile Court, whether criminal or civil, are not open to the public; restrictions are placed on the classes of persons entitled to attend,[6] and on the publication of reports[7] by the media which might lead to the identification of the child.

The chairman of the bench

In court, one of the Justices holds the position of chairman.[8] The chairman is recognised as 'first among equals': although he does not possess any special powers over his colleagues (since the decision of the court is reached by a majority verdict), yet his is a position of dignity and responsibility, and the reputation of the bench can depend greatly on his handling of any court situation.

He is essentially the spokesman for the bench (though this does not debar the other Justices from putting questions to anyone giving evidence) and in the final analysis he controls the conduct of the court.

The conduct of a case, whether in criminal or care proceedings, is clearly defined in the Magistrates' Courts (Children and Young Persons) Rules 1970, as amended by the Magistrates' Courts (Children and Young Persons) (Amendment) Rules 1976, and these should be closely studied by the social worker.

In brief the chairman, as spokesman for the court, should endeavour to ensure that both parent and child understand all that is taking place throughout the hearing and he should clarify any matter which calls for explanation. After the hearing of a case it is his duty to declare the finding of the court, and give the parent or guardian of the child an opportunity to make a statement or representation to the court.

Any order which the court decides upon should be carefully explained to the child, unless this is considered inexpedient.[9] It is the responsibility of the bench to ensure that proceedings are made as simple and intelligible as possible so that neither parent, guardian nor child is confused. In the case of a child who is in the care of a Local Authority, that Authority is his guardian, and the social worker as agent for the Authority has the right to address the court or make representation in appropriate cases.[10]

The Magistrates' Court and lay magistrates

Lay magistrates (Justices of the Peace) are so called to differentiate between them and stipendiary magistrates. A number of stipendiaries are appointed in Metropolitan Areas to sit in Magistrates' Courts; they are paid for the office they hold. They are legally trained, can sit in court alone, and in effect can conduct a case in the lower court as does a judge in the higher court, except that there is no jury to direct, and findings of guilt or otherwise are made by the stipendiary himself. In areas where both stipendiary and lay magistrates are appointed, it is reasonably safe to say that the stipendiary will deal with the more serious cases. When he sits with lay magistrates, however, his powers are no greater than theirs, except that he usually occupies the position of chairman.

The Magistrates' Court, like the Juvenile Court, is a Court of Summary Jurisdiction, which requires the presence of two or more magistrates. The greatest number permitted to sit is seven but it is recommended that three is more appropriate for the dispensation of justice, and where possible the court should include a woman.

Jurisdiction in the Magistrates' Court is very much wider than in the Juvenile Court, but for the purpose of this manual a broad division may be drawn to cover criminal and civil proceedings.

Criminal proceedings

Criminal proceedings are a very important feature of the magistrates' work, as more than 90 per cent of all criminal actions are heard in the Magistrates' Court. The process of a case will be examined in Chapter 3. Lay magistrates are empowered to try all minor offences, but some of these are quite serious and are also indictable. This means they could be tried in a higher court, and that after trial and examination of the offender's antecedents, a committal to the Crown Court for sentence may be ordered. This is because the magistrates' sentencing powers may be inadequate.

Sentencing powers in the Magistrates' Court are much greater than in the Juvenile Court, and though discussion of sentences has been avoided here, a knowledge of them is valuable, particularly when a probation officer or social worker is preparing a social enquiry report to assist the court in its final disposal of a case.

The function of the chairman in both courts is similar, except that in the Magistrates' Court he is not expected to explain proceedings to the defendant nor is he under any obligation to give an explanation of the verdict of the court. He will however clarify the terms and effects of any sentence or conditions made by the court.

In any case which *must* be tried in a higher court, where the court decides committal for trial is necessary, or an offender elects for trial by jury on an indictable offence, the Justices act as *examining magistrates*.

In such cases it is their duty to examine the evidence to decide if there is a prima case to answer; if there is they commit to the Crown Court for trial. Should the court decide there is no case to answer then the charge against the offender must be dismissed.

It may be well to remember that neither the Juvenile Court nor the Magistrates' Court can sentence an offender to Borstal training. If such a course is considered by either court there must be a committal to the Crown Court for sentencing, and, with some exceptions, before any custodial sentence is passed by the lower courts a social enquiry report should be requested.

Civil proceedings

The Magistrates' Court covers a wider range of civil proceedings than the Juvenile Court and those which could affect the social worker or probation officer are noted in Chapters 8 to 10. These proceedings will be heard in the Domestic Court.

Prior to the Domestic Proceedings and Magistrates' Courts Act 1978, it was possible for any Justice to sit in the Domestic Court, but section 80 of the Act provides that no Justice can sit in the Domestic Court unless he is a member of a Domestic Court Panel (that is, a panel of Justices specially appointed to deal with domestic proceedings). This is yet to be enacted.

Domestic proceedings cover a wide range of enactments including matrimonial matters, affiliation, guardianship of minors, maintenance, custody, custodianship and adoption. Unlike criminal proceedings in the Magistrates' Court which are public hearings, domestic proceedings are not open to the general public. As in the Juvenile Court, restrictions are placed on the classes of persons permitted to attend and on the reporting of certain matters by the media.[11]

Space does not permit the detailing of all the procedures in a Domestic Court but those relevant to social workers and probation officers will be noted in later chapters.

The Justices' Clerk

In law, it is the Justices who constitute a Magistrates' Court, and this of course includes the Juvenile Court. However, as all Justices are not trained nor expert in legal matters, they are assisted by a Justices' Clerk or clerk of the court. The Justices' Clerk is the chief clerk who is responsible for all court transactions and business, and although he himself may sit with the Justices, very often it is someone junior to him who sits as clerk of the court.

The court can, however, seek the advice of the Justices' Clerk at all times, though not on the appropriateness of a sentence. The legal knowledge (or access to it) and expertise of the clerk, his participation in the proceedings and the support he offers are complementary to the work of the Justices. As the Juvenile Court is more informal than other courts (with the possible exception of the Domestic Court), and unrepresented children less capable of presenting evidence or cross-examining witnesses, there is a general tendency for the clerk in the Juvenile Court to take a more active part in the proceedings.

In most cases, he puts the charge or complaint to the child in terms which can be readily understood, and assists him with the case in so far as it is practicable and within the scope of the law.

His main function, however, is to give advice to the Justices on matters pertaining to law, practice and procedure, and at any stage in the proceedings to bring to the notice of the Justices any relevant points of law as he thinks appropriate.

He can refresh their memory on any matter presented in evidence, for example, by referring to notes taken during the hearing of a case, and he can acquaint them of their sentencing powers, on the general level of fines for particular offences, and any appropriate matters on which they require his advice in order to make correct decisions.

He cannot take part in the actual decision of a case. The finding of fact and the making of an order are entirely the responsibility of the Justices and they must carry out their duty in this respect. The Practice Division of the High Court has made it clear that under no circumstances may the Justices consult their clerk as to the guilt or innocence of the defendant. It is the Justices who constitute the court, and they alone must decide the issue of a case. Having decided the issue they must then decide on the appropriate order or sentence.

The other duties of a Justices' Clerk are quite extensive, and for those interested they are detailed in the Justices' Clerk Rules 1970 as amended.

A view is held that the clerk should not examine witnesses who are legally represented, nor any party who although unrepresented is competent and desires to examine the witness himself. However, where the unrepresented party, whoever he may be, is not competent (through lack of knowledge of court procedure or rules of evidence or otherwise) to examine the witness properly, the court may at its discretion permit the clerk to do so.

In the Juvenile Court setting most children and parents are quite incompetent to carry out the cross-examination of witnesses, and where they are unrepresented this is frequently undertaken by the clerk.

A local authority social worker, as agent for the Authority, could undertake the cross-examination of witnesses on behalf of a child in care, but unfortunately too few are competent to do so.

As with Justices, impartiality is, or should be, one of the hallmarks of the clerk. It should be said in conclusion that most clerks will and do give valuable assistance to social workers, probation officers and others involved in the work of the court. Indeed, a good relationship with the clerk can lead to a similar situation with the Justices and should at all times be encouraged.

3. The Prosecutor and Advocate for the Defence

In this chapter we shall consider the roles of the prosecutor and the advocate for the defence in criminal proceedings, and follow this by looking at the applicant, complainant and respondent or defendant in civil cases.

The basic difference between criminal and civil proceedings is that the former are instituted under state or public law and the latter under private law.

Public law is concerned with the relationship between an individual and the rest of the community as a whole. Private law concerns the relationships between individuals in that community in so far as they do not involve or concern the community as a whole.[1]

In the criminal court the prosecution has to prove that an offence has been committed by the defendant; in the civil court the defendant (or respondent, as he is often called) has to defend himself against a complaint made about him. Thus in care proceedings, for instance, the child as respondent has to defend himself against the claim of the Local Authority that he comes under the category of one of the specific conditions stated in section 1 of the Children and Young Persons Act 1969 and that he is in need of care and control which can only be exercised through a court order.

Criminal proceedings

The prosecutor

The *prosecutor* is the person who, in effect, sets the proceedings in motion. This he does by way of a charge, information, summons or warrant.

He is the accuser, the one who alleges that an offence has been committed by a named person or persons; as such he is responsible for proving his case against the accused. He must establish proof beyond reasonable doubt, and failure to do so means the accused must be acquitted.

The only way in which a case can be proved in court is through the *presentation of evidence*: this term is used to indicate the method adopted for sifting out the truth of an issue in accordance with the law of evidence. Witnesses are called and placed on oath or affirmation to tell the truth, the whole truth and nothing but the truth of any facts they know, or to produce documents, articles, etc., which have a definite bearing on the case. Under the guidance of the prosecutor, the witness gives his evidence; this is commonly known as *examination-in-chief*. He is then *cross-examined* by the defendant or his advocate, and finally may be *re-examined* by the prosecutor who may wish to clarify or emphasise any particular factors brought out in the cross-examination.

The *examination-in-chief* is the examination of a witness by the party who produces him, and is also called *direct examination*.[2]

During this examination, the examiner (be he prosecutor or advocate for the defence) must not put *leading questions* to the witness, nor allow him to give *hearsay evidence*. The opposing side may object to either of these and appeal to the court to intervene. A *leading question* is one which contains or suggests the answer desired on a vital point, and if admitted could possibly lead to a miscarriage of justice. *Hearsay evidence* is evidence of a fact which is not actually known to the witness but was disclosed to him by another person. The disclosure may be accurate but the witness has no proof that it is, and therefore he cannot on oath so testify.

The *cross-examination* follows direct examination and offers the other party the opportunity to examine the witness on the evidence he has given, and so to test and perhaps break down the credibility of his testimony.

In this examination, leading questions can be asked, and if there is any doubt about the honesty of the witness, this too can be challenged in an effort to discredit his evidence.

Where the examination relates to the character of the defendant, questions which suggest that this might be bad or doubtful can only be put to him if he has claimed to be of good character during the course of his examination-in-chief, or if he has attacked the character of a witness.

After cross-examination the party who called the witness can *re-examine* him in relation to new facts which may have been brought out during the cross-examination, or in order to clarify or explain any part of this.

Parents and children often find difficulty in understanding all these processes, and social workers with a sound working knowledge of the court could probably help their clients in this respect. Some indication of what to expect before appearing in court may alleviate the stress of being confronted by a strange situation, which so often unsettles those involved in the proceedings.

The essence of good examination-in-chief is to draw out the strength of a case against the other party, and that of good cross-examination to exploit every weakness in the testimony given, either to destroy it or cast doubt upon it.

The perfect witness

He should relate in ordinary language the story he can tell of his own knowledge as to what he has seen, heard, etc. He should confine himself to facts, avoiding inferences, opinions or beliefs. He should tell his story in the natural order and sequence of events as they occurred. He should speak from memory, expressing himself clearly and accurately. He should not produce his notebook as a matter of course and read out all his evidence therefrom. If he finds it necessary to refresh his memory he may be allowed to consult his notes. When asked a question, he should listen carefully to the question, make sure he understands it, and give an intelligent and proper answer to the best of his ability. He should only answer the questions put to him, and then, in as few words as possible, promptly and frankly. He should never lose his temper under cross-examination, and should always reply politely and quietly to offensive questions.

He should not show partisanship or prejudice, and ought to give his evidence fairly and impartially, giving all the evidence in favour of the accused in addition to the evidence against him. He is sworn to tell the truth, the whole truth and nothing but the truth.[3]

The police, who are so frequently the prosecutors in criminal proceedings, are among the few who are actually taught to give evidence. While it would be foolish to suggest that they always practise what they are taught, nevertheless they are generally the most adept witnesses in presenting evidence and facing cross-examination.

Social workers, who have to act in the capacity of chief witness when they or their Authority are acting in the role of prosecutor or defendant, should learn the precepts of the perfect witness. No one can deny that the better the evidence is presented, the more effective the result, in most issues.

As the burden of proof is on the prosecutor, it is he who presents his case first, and if he proves there is a prima facie case to answer, then the defence presents its case in a similar manner. At the conclusion of the evidence, the prosecutor will make a final speech going over the strength of the evidence in his favour to prove his case. The defendant or his advocate will reply in an effort to refute or discredit the prosecutor's case.

If he can cast a reasonable doubt on the prosecution's accusation, and this is accepted by the court, the case against the defendant must be dismissed. It is for the court to decide whether or not there is a reasonable doubt, after careful consideration of all the evidence from both parties. If, in the opinion of the court, the prosecutor has proved his case beyond all reasonable doubt, then a verdict of guilty must be recorded against the defendant. The defendant may make a mitigating plea, and then an appropriate order must be made, either following the verdict or, when reports have been requested to assist the Justices in their final disposal of the case, after a period on remand.

The defendant and his advocate

The *defendant* is a person accused by another of committing an offence which, if this accusation is proved to be correct, renders him liable to a penalty, varying in intensity according to the gravity of the offence and the antecedents of the offender.

This is an invidious position to be in, and to offer him some protection the law provides that he must be considered innocent until proved guilty.

To avoid any possibility of unfairness during his trial, any indication of previous bad character must be omitted from the evidence against him, except when in the course of his own evidence he attacks the character of a witness, or sets himself up to be a person of good character. Under such circumstances his character may be attacked under cross-examination.

He has every legal right to conduct his own defence, but can choose to be legally represented by engaging a solicitor himself, or through application to the court to be granted legal aid (that is, financial help towards representation by a solicitor of his choice). This may in some cases lead to representation by counsel. Social workers should be prepared to advise children and their parents on this matter, and take pains themselves to know what can and should be done at any time.

The defence follows the same lines as the prosecution in that witnesses can be called to give evidence on behalf of the defendant, or to produce documents, articles, etc., which may be relevant to the case and of assistance to the defendant.

The defendant or his advocate will guide each witness through the examination-in-chief, the prosecutor will then cross-examine the witness, and finally the defendant (or his advocate, if he so desires) will re-examine each witness (including the defendant if he gives evidence) to clear up matters raised in cross-examination.

There is no statutory duty placed on the defendant to give evidence on his own behalf. Three options are open to him:

(a)   he need say nothing at all,
(b)   he can make a statement without going into the witness box, or
(c)   he can give evidence on oath or by affirmation.

If he chooses to make a statement he cannot be questioned by the prosecution or the court. This means, however, that there will be no way of testing the truth of his statement, a factor which will not be lost on the Justices. In giving evidence on oath or by affirmation he can be cross-examined by the prosecutor and the weight of his evidence fully tested. In most charges, particularly those of a serious nature, the latter course is adopted, and normally after the prosecution's case has been presented the defendant gives his own evidence which is followed by the evidence of his witnesses.

When all the evidence is given on both sides, final speeches are generally made, first by the prosecutor and then by the defendant or his advocate. The court considers all the evidence heard and returns a verdict. If the verdict is 'not guilty' the defendant is acquitted, but if the decision is 'guilty', the court must give the defendant or his advocate the opportunity of addressing the Justices, mainly to present a plea of mitigation. The antecedents of the defendant are then given to the court and a sentence (or in the Juvenile Court, an order) imposed, or a remand for a social enquiry or other reports ordered.

Civil proceedings

In civil proceedings the *applicant* or *complainant* is the party who brings a complaint, or matter to be judged, before a court. The *respondent* is the person who challenges that complaint. These brief definitions may assist in understanding the roles of the opposing parties in civil cases.

The applicant in care proceedings

In care proceedings, in which the social worker is most frequently involved, only four parties have the authority to be applicants, namely:

(a)   the police,
(b)   a Local Authority,
(c)   a Local Education Authority,
(d)   the NSPCC.

In accordance with section 2 (8) of the Children and Young Persons Act 1969, only the Local Education Authority can institute care proceedings on non-attendance at school and other prescribed educational matters, but it cannot bring any child before a Juvenile Court on any of the other conditions set out in section 1 of that Act.

The NSPCC has no power to act in relation to the educational test nor in respect of the offence condition, but it is empowered to initiate proceedings on the other specified conditions in section 1 (2) (a to d). In doing so it must notify the appropriate Local Authority of its intentions.

The Local Authority and the police, whose powers are greatest under the 1969 Act, can institute proceedings in all specified conditions with the exception of the education test, though in all matters the police must notify the Local Authority of any action to be taken. Although the Local Authority has no power of action on the education test it may be very much involved in the proceedings, both in assisting to prove that the care and control test is satisfied, and in preparing reports for the court which may lead to a supervision or care order.

The making of an application by an authorised applicant, and also the progress of a case in court, are defined by the Magistrates' Courts (Children and Young Persons) Rules 1970 as amended by the Amendment Rules of 1976. The conduct of a case by an applicant is similar to that by a prosecutor, and involves the examination of witnesses, cross-examination and re-examination on both sides – the applicant and the respondent.

If the complaint sets out to prove that the offence condition is satisfied, the standard of proof required is the same as that in criminal proceedings: the offence must be proved beyond reasonable doubt.

Although the burden of proof rests with the applicant in the offence condition, there are occasions when the onus of proof shifts to the respondent, as in criminal proceedings. For instance, if the offence were that of driving without a licence, the applicant might prove there was a prima facie case to answer by establishing the fact that no licence was produced when requested. It would then be the responsibility of the respondent (defendant) to prove that he had a licence at the time of the alleged offence, by producing it in evidence. (Any licence produced must of course cover the period in which the offence was alleged to have been committed.) Failure to prove ownership of a current licence would result in the offence condition being proved.

Apart from the offence condition, all other conditions are satisfied on the balance of probabilities, a factor which applies to all civil proceedings. The reason for this is that they are based not only on what has happened, but also on what is likely to happen in the future. Facts are essential in proving any specified condition but, unlike the situation which obtains in criminal proceedings, they can be substantiated by hearsay evidence, and the proof demanded need not be 'beyond reasonable doubt'.

The complainant in section 2 resolutions

Under section 2 of the Children Act 1948 (as substituted by section 57 of the Children Act 1975) a Local Authority is empowered to pass a resolution assuming parental rights over a child who is in care under section 1 of the 1948 Act. Within a month of a notice being served on a parent, guardian or custodian, informing him of the resolution, he can object to the Local Authority in writing. If the Authority fails to take action within fourteen days of receiving the written objection, then the resolution must lapse.

Before the expiry of the fourteen days, however, the Local Authority can bring the matter to the notice of the appropriate Juvenile Court by way of complaint. A date is then set for a hearing of the complaint which follows similar lines to other civil proceedings.

The resolution remains until the court makes a decision, following the evidence presented by the *complainant* (the Local Authority) and the *respondent* (the parent, etc.).

The complainant must prove to the court that one of the situations specified in section 57 of the Children Act 1975 applies to the respondent, and this may require careful investigation on the part of the social worker. It must be shown that the child was in care under section 1 of the Children Act 1948 when the resolution was passed, though probably executed following a request of the parent for the return of the child. The grounds for passing the resolution must be well substantiated, as they suggest serious defects in a parent which should be most carefully analysed.

The applicant in adoption proceedings

The *applicant* in an adoption hearing is the person applying to adopt a child, and the *respondent* is a person to whom a notice is sent under section 12 of the Adoption Act 1958 (as amended by the Adoption Rules 1976, for High Court, County Court and Magistrates' Court). The proceedings are at present heard in the Juvenile Court, but arrangements have been made for them to be transferred to the Domestic Court as domestic proceedings in accordance with the Domestic Proceedings and Magistrates' Courts Act 1978, section 79.

There is much to be done by the applicant and the respondent, including the appropriate Local Authority, before the matter comes to the court for a final decision, and the social worker can be very much involved with the legal and other preliminaries entailed in adoption welfare and guardian *ad litem* duties.

The majority of adoption cases are decided on an amicable basis, as in most instances both the applicant and respondent, even though unknown to each other, have chosen that the child be grafted into a new family which they hope will fulfil all his needs.

Matrimonial proceedings in the Domestic Court

Matrimonial proceedings in the Domestic Court will soon be brought into line with proceedings in other courts as a result of the Domestic Proceedings and Magistrates' Courts Act 1978 which replaces the Matrimonial Proceedings (Magistrates' Courts) Act 1960 (see page 50).

In these proceedings the term *applicant* refers to a person making a complaint against a spouse, or applying for a matrimonial order or revocation or variation of an order. It may include a grandparent applying for access to grandchildren, particularly in relation to a matrimonial order made by the court. The term *respondent* refers to the person answering the complaint or opposing the application.

Proceedings are instituted by way of a summons in which one of the spouses registers a complaint against the other, and the case can only be heard if the summons is properly served. In some cases the matter can be heard when only one party is present, where the other shows no desire to attend. Where both parties appear, however, the conduct of the proceedings is similar to the others previously described.

The representative for the applicant makes a speech outlining the facts, and then calls witnesses to verify these facts. Each witness called can be cross-examined and then re-examined.

When the applicant's evidence is completed, the respondent and his witnesses then give evidence, which can also be cross-examined and re-examined.

The representative for the respondent will then address the magistrates on behalf of the respondent. If his speech includes one or more points of law, the opposing representative can make a further speech dealing only with the points of law raised.

The social worker's involvement in these proceedings is likely to be limited to the preparation of reports at the request of the court.

Guardianship proceedings

The *applicant* in these proceedings is the person who is applying for the custody of a child, where the application is opposed, the other party is the *respondent*.

The effective Acts in these cases are the Guardianship of Minors Act 1971 and the Guardianship Act 1973 as amended by the Domestic Proceedings and Magistrates' Courts Act 1978.

The procedure does not differ greatly from other proceedings in the Domestic Court, with the exception that the magistrates are seeking evidence which will enable them to decide whether a person should be given custody of a child (or in a contested case between two parents, which parent should have custody). They may, of course, decide that neither party should have custody, and instead give custody to a third party or commit the child to the care of a Local Authority.

In their deliberations the magistrates must regard the welfare of the child as the first consideration, a factor of considerable importance to the social worker or probation officer should either be requested to prepare reports for the court.

Custodianship proceedings

Custodianship is a new concept in child legislation, introduced by the Children Act 1975 but not yet operative. It is discussed more fully in Chapter 7.

When implemented, these proceedings are likely to involve the social worker quite extensively, and though rules have not been drawn up at the time of writing, they will probably fall very much in line with guardianship proceedings.

Custodianship increases the number of persons qualified to apply for legal custody of a child and undoubtedly must add to the social worker's already onerous task.

When adoption hearings are transferred to the Domestic Court and custodianship orders introduced, it becomes easy to visualise Social Services Departments playing an important role in all aspects of the work of the Domestic Court.

There is much therefore for social workers to learn about courts other than Juvenile Courts, and the roles they may be expected to play.

4. The Role of the Police

The general view of the police is that their sole task is to root out crime and bring the criminal to justice. Many people, including some social workers, see them as punitive in outlook, with little understanding of the inner conflicts and problems of those they bring to court.

However, within the court setting and in the work leading to court proceedings, the police have much in common with the social worker: a greater realisation of this may lead them to a more effective relationship with each other. Unfortunately, their approach and attitude to the work often differs, and this frequently leads to criticism and counter-criticism. Much of this might be averted by closer co-operation and communication: the Children and Young Persons Act 1969, which they are both expected to implement, is geared to this.

The common denominators in their work are clearly indicated in child legislation. All offences committed by or against children and young persons may be the subject of court proceedings, as can care proceedings in which the interests and the future of the young are very much at stake.

Thus both police and social workers may be called upon to act as prosecutors, applicants, defendants, respondents or witnesses in cases relating to children or young persons. There may be occasions when they are in opposing camps, but neither should lose sight of the main purpose of any Juvenile Court proceedings, as set out in the Children and Young Persons Act 1933, section 44: 'Every court in dealing with a child or young person who is brought before it, either as an offender or otherwise, shall have regard to the welfare of the child or young person and shall in a proper case take steps for removing him from undesirable surroundings and for securing that proper provision is made for his education and training.'

This makes it clear that the welfare of the child is more important than the offence (which may be doubted) but does not exclude the need to consider the interests of the public.

Under section 59 of the Children Act 1975, the Local Authority has a duty, when reaching a decision with regard to a child in care, to give first consideration to the need to safeguard and promote the welfare of the child throughout his childhood. However, in accordance with that same section, if the Authority considers it necessary, for the purpose of protecting members of the public, to act in a way which is not consistent with that recognised duty, it must do so.

The court has to operate along similar lines, and may have to take a course which is not totally consistent with the child's welfare but is a protection to the public.

Preserving a balance between the child's interests and those of the public is not always easy, and there are no guide-lines set out to simplify the position for Justices, police, social workers, probation officers and others. This lack of direction may mean that conflicting points of view create friction between those dealing with the child or young person.

This matter cannot be dealt with in depth here, but in the broadest terms it may be said that the child's interests relate to his growth and development in all aspects of his life, and those of the public to their personal protection and the protection of their property.

Freedom, for instance, is or should be the right of all; but if freedom is to be enjoyed by all it must have restrictions, otherwise it leads to licence or anarchy. In dealing with a child or young person who is building up a delinquent reputation, one must consider what damage he is doing to himself and others (and what damage others might do to him), and carefully decide whether it is in his or their interests for him to remain where he is. It may be necessary to deprive him of his present freedom to ensure an alternative freedom which will help in his proper growth and development.

Although the Local Authority has power to prosecute in criminal proceedings, nevertheless it is invariably left to the police to do so. In dealing with the more hardened criminals in particular, both juvenile and adult, they are often forced into the position of being punitive in outlook, viewing this as being a realistic attitude in dealing with crime.

Social workers, on the other hand, deal more with the institution of care proceedings, which savour less of punishment. Their approach is thought of as 'treatment', a term which is at best defined only vaguely. In fact for many young people a removal from home is a form of punishment, no matter what terminology is used. It is no bad thing to remember that the distinction between 'treatment' and 'punishment' may well depend on whether you are administering or receiving it.

Punitive measures have not proved to be the sole answer to delinquency, and neither have the so-called therapeutic approaches, although the individual delinquent or criminal may respond to one or the other at different times; hence the impossibility of generalising.

In genuine efforts to help the difficult young offender (who undoubtedly is the cause of all the furore surrounding the 1969 Act, and whose needs are probably the greatest), it may be that too much time is spent on theorising, and too little spent in obtaining a fuller understanding of the young delinquent. This might well lead to more constructive and success-ful methods – though it may be *people* rather than methods which are needed. Perhaps we should view the offender less as a clinical curiosity, and more as a human being who needs help and support from someone he can trust and respect.

A fuller composite picture can only be built up through co-operation and consultation with all those involved with the young person, and particularly with the police and the social worker. It is important that they break down the barrier which frequently holds them back from positive communication with each other.

It is obvious from the nature and pressures of their work that police and social workers cannot arrange consultations on every child appearing before the court, and both must have freedom and scope to work inde-pendently of each other. There is, however, always a small number of difficult youngsters who require the concerted efforts of the police, social worker, probation officer, magistrate and others.

In the HMSO document 'Part 1 of the Children and Young Persons Act, 1969' (a guide and reference booklet for practitioners on the sub-stantive provisions of the Act), emphasis is laid on police and social worker consultation and a quotation from this may well be worthy of attention.

> The Act leaves it entirely to the police forces and Local Authorities in each area to work out their own arrangements for consultation. . . . An important consideration is the degree of selectivity there should be in the consultation arrangements. Manpower considerations are likely to make it impractical to consult on all cases before deciding what action if any to take when a child is in trouble. An attempt to consult on all cases without exception would be likely to stretch the available man-power unduly, and thus to mean that fewer resources were available to deal with the more difficult cases for which they were most needed.
>
> The Act does not affect the discretion of the police officer to decide to take no action at all, or to give a child an informal warning on the spot, or to give a formal caution, without consulting the Local Authority. It may be desirable, in order that local authority manpower may be concentrated on cases where their help is most needed and that deci-sions may be taken as quickly as is reasonably practical, for the police to do some preliminary sifting and make some preliminary enquiries, and for the depth of consultation to vary according to the need for it.

If greater efforts to co-operate were made, and better methods of consul-tation adopted, then there might be less feeling of hostility in particularly difficult cases in which the police and the social worker are involved in court. Consultation between the police and the social worker is not, of course, a universal panacea for juvenile delinquency, but it could help to break down the prejudices of both parties, and lead to a more concerted effort to work out possible solutions. It must be emphasised that not all social workers are opposed to appropriate punitive measures, nor are all policemen advocates of punishment whatever the circumstances. Custodial sentences can in some cases prove beneficial to the young offender (and also to adults), but they should not, in my opinion, be linked with rejection. Rejection can be much more damaging than punishment, as many ex-prisoners have discovered. I would suggest, for example, that where a residential social worker recommends a custodial order, it should rarely if ever be with the rider that the offender may not return to that establishment. If the social worker demonstrates a readiness to accept the return of the young offender after completion of his custodial order, the young person is helped to appreciate that tough action taken in his interest is not a signal of rejection but a genuine effort to safeguard his future. It has been known for such action to strengthen rather than weaken relationships.

It is not suggested that the outcome will always be successful, but the prospects for the future are often brighter.

The Juvenile Bureau

In many areas a Juvenile Bureau, staffed by non-uniformed police officers, has been set up to deal with juvenile offenders and to decide whether to warn, caution or prosecute the child or young person who admits to the commission of an offence. Though the uniformed police need not proceed through the bureau in every case, the normal practice in the Metropolitan Police District of London is for them to investigate an offence initially and pass the offender over to the bureau.

An officer of the bureau then makes investigations which entail:

(a) Establishing a prima facie case against the juvenile. This is readily achieved when the child or young person openly admits to the commission of an offence.

(b) Contact with the Local Authority Social Services Department, either in writing or through a visit to the department's office. In this connection enquiries are made to ascertain if the juvenile is known to the services, what information can be given which may prove valuable in the recommendation of appropriate action, and what views the social worker may have on the matter.

(c) A request for information from the local Education Department or school about the juvenile and his parents or guardian, to obtain some indication of the family background, home surroundings, attitudes

within the family and relationships with siblings, peers and associates.

(e)   Consideration of all the information gathered, assessment of the situation in the light of this and recommendation on the action considered appropriate. This is presented to the Chief Inspector of the bureau, who will decide whether to warn, caution or prosecute.

If the decision is to prosecute, the matter will then go back to the uniformed police who will set proceedings in motion and conduct the prosecution. The bureau does not act as prosecutor.

The purpose of the bureau is laudable, and it appears to operate reasonably satisfactorily, though it has its critics within the police force and from outside sources. Some people see it as a quasi social work agency which weakens the effectiveness of the force. Many social workers view it as an amateur social work agency endeavouring to perform a task which should be left to trained and skilled social workers. Many criticise the bureau because its mode of practice differs throughout the country and it is too secretive in some areas: this provokes doubts about its dealings with some juveniles.

Perhaps the main criticism which can be readily aimed at the bureau is the delay it creates in bringing juveniles before the court. The purpose of the 1969 Act is to ensure, as far as possible, that no juvenile should have the trauma of a court appearance hanging over his head for an unnecessarily lengthy period. The bureau would no doubt argue that on the other hand its painstaking care before deciding on a course of action minimises court appearances, and this is beneficial to the juvenile.

If the police institute proceedings by way of a charge (normally on serious offences) this does *not* proceed through the bureau. Under such circumstances the juvenile is brought before the court immediately or within seventy-two hours.

Where proceedings are instituted as a result of the bureau's recommendation, this is initiated by way of a summons, or in certain circumstances by issue of a warrant. The purpose of a summons or warrant is to ensure the attendance in court of the relevant party or parties. This may include parents, guardians, the child or young person, and in some circumstances witnesses or others.

There is, however, no obligation to serve notice, summons or warrant on a parent or guardian who through a court order has been deprived of custody of a child or young person (as, for example, when he is committed to the care of a Local Authority through a care order, or custody has been given to another person).

5. The Social Worker as Applicant, Witness and Advocate

The earlier outlines of the roles involved in court proceedings enable us to examine more closely the various roles of the social worker. Some of these are equally the province of the probation officer, with certain appreciable differences in approach and attitudes. (Further roles of the latter are set out in Chapter 9.)

There may be considerable value in pointing out that the social worker acts primarily as representative of his Local Authority. Indeed, this is interwoven with every other role undertaken in or for the court, and it should be considered carefully and seriously by every worker.

Social workers frequently register complaints against the employing Authority on innumerable premises, particularly in relation to the limitations of finance and the shortage of facilities, which militate against the accomplishment of the professional task for which the worker is trained. Complaints and criticisms can be valuable, and often need to be vigorously pursued in order to achieve improvement in the work and conditions of service. Legitimate as his grievances against the Authority may be, however, the social worker should always remember that when in court he acts on its behalf.

Within the court setting the social worker has the responsibility of presenting his Authority's viewpoint. What he says is the voice of his Authority, what he decides is its decision and what he recommends is its recommendation. A care order recommended by the social worker places the Authority *in loco parentis*, and the grave responsibilities attached to this position continue with the Authority until the order is revoked or has run its course. The Authority must be able to trust its officers and that trust should not be abused. With this important observation we can now turn to the social worker's roles in court.

The role of applicant in care proceedings

One of the most familiar roles of the social worker in the court setting is that of applicant in care proceedings. The normal procedure in most

Authorities is for the case to be brought before the court by a legal representative of the Authority, but all or most of the background information is gathered by the social worker. It may be helpful to consider a possible sequence of events.

As a result of a referral from one source or another, the worker is alerted to the fact that a child is being ill-treated, is exposed to moral danger, is beyond the control of a parent or guardian, or that any other of the primary conditions (as set out in section 1 of the Children and Young Persons Act 1969) may be satisfied.

Investigation of the matter confirms the social worker's view that there is reasonable ground for believing that the child is in need of care and control which he cannot receive unless the court makes an order.

It is considered advisable that the child be removed from home, and in consultation with a senior officer a decision is made to apply for a place of safety order.[1] A Justice is approached, an outline of the situation presented to him, and if he is satisfied that there are reasonable grounds for the request, he grants and signs the appropriate order.

After the various documents and arrangements are completed, the child is removed from home and taken to a place of safety which normally is a suitable establishment, provided by or on behalf of the Local Authority. This may be a community home, a voluntary home, a hospital or any other suitable place which is willing temporarily to receive the child.[2]

Simultaneously, if the parents are available, or later when they can be found, they are given a copy of the order, and told in simple language the reason for the action taken. This may meet with a very mixed reception, depending upon the character of the parents, and in some cases (fortunately very few) the removal of the child may be quite impossible without police assistance.

With all the initial processes completed, the social worker now has twenty-eight days (or a lesser period, as decided by the Justice) to investigate the full circumstances of the child, the parents and family background, and to make one of three decisions:

(a)   to return the child to his parents within the period of the order,
(b)   to receive the child into care under section 1 of the Children Act 1948, *with the consent of the parents*, or
(c)   to institute care proceedings within the twenty-eight days or the period granted by the Justice.

In contemplating care proceedings, the social worker must be aware of the fact that two conditions (the primary and secondary conditions) must be proved in court. The terms used here are adopted from the HMSO booklet 'Part 1 of the Children and Young Persons Act 1969'. The *primary condition* is one of the separate conditions set out in sub-section 2 of section 1 of the Act: these are generally accepted as warranting social intervention. On the weight of the evidence given the court must be convinced that the condition is satisfied in respect of the child, but it cannot make an order on that factor alone.

In addition to proving the primary condition, the applicant must also prove to the court that the child is in need of care and control which he is unlikely to receive unless the court makes an order. This is the *secondary condition*.

Appreciating this fact, it is imperative that the social worker has early and detailed consultations with his superior and the legal representative, and that throughout the duration of the place of safety order there is a careful and painstaking collection and preparation of evidence. This is essential in deciding whether there are grounds for proceedings and in ensuring that a proper case will be presented to court.

Care proceedings should never be taken lightly. They can deprive a child of his freedom or his family, or take away the parental rights of a parent or guardian; they therefore place a heavy burden of responsibility on the applicant who brings the child before a court. The far-reaching effects must be considered seriously and conscientiously, and much time and effort should be expended in investigating, methodically and efficiently, all the circumstances of a case. This also applies to the preparation of social enquiry reports, discussed in Chapter 6.

Where grounds exist for the institution of care proceedings, and the social worker in consultation with his senior decides that they should be initiated, then the legal representative will make the necessary application to the court, and notify all appropriate respondents of the date, time and place of the hearing.

The social worker as chief witness

In court the legal representative for the Local Authority will conduct the case for the applicant and call on witnesses to give evidence.

The social worker will be treated as his chief witness and probably also as a specialist witness. It will be necessary therefore for him to establish his credibility as a witness, giving some indication of his qualifications and experience, as well as his present position, and the length of time he has been associated with the case. He will be guided by the legal representative through the evidence he has carefully prepared (in the examination-in-chief), and from this will seek to establish that the primary condition is satisfied in respect of the child.

The evidence given by the social worker should be of a high standard (like that of the perfect witness as outlined in Chapter 3). It should be delivered with absolute impartiality, and demonstrate a readiness to speak in favour of the child or his parents as well as against them.

In care proceedings the child's welfare is more important than the winning or losing of a case; but inevitably the social worker is anxious to be successful in his cause and will be deflated by any other result. All verdicts do not go in favour of the social worker, and this is a fact which must be accepted with some grace, together with the possibility that in some cases the court may be right and the social worker wrong. The court has a duty to give first consideration to the child's welfare. When judgement is made in a contested case, the court must judge in accordance with the law; even where the Justices may have sympathy with a cause they can do nothing if the cause is not legally proved.

Evidence given in court will be thoroughly tested before judgement can be given; therefore it must be carefully prepared and assembled, and clearly and confidently stated in court. It is most essential for the social worker, as chief witness, to listen very carefully to any question he is asked, to make sure he understands it (seeking clarification when there is any vagueness about it) and answer clearly. Clarity and brevity in answering questions, especially under cross-examination, is normally more effective than lengthy exposition. Any weakness in a protracted answer will be quickly spotted and worked upon by a good legal opponent.

Although the standard of proof in care proceedings is not so demanding as that in criminal proceedings (with the exception of the offence condition), nevertheless the best evidence which can be given by the witness is that which he can tell of his own knowledge of what he has heard or seen, etc. This undoubtedly carries most weight in court.

After the applicant and respondent have completed their evidence for the court, and concluding addresses have been made by their representatives, the court will weigh up the evidence and decide whether or not the primary condition is satisfied in respect of the child. If it is, then it is necessary for the applicant to prove the secondary condition (the care or control test), and show that care or control can only be achieved if the court makes an order. The evidence necessary for this can be given orally or by way of a written report prepared by the social worker. This should be open to question by the respondent.

It appears, from the Children and Young Persons Act 1969, that the primary and secondary conditions are two separate issues, both of which must be proved before the court can make an order. However, in some courts it is doubtful whether the issues are separated as clearly as they should be, and the impression is frequently given that if the primary condition is satisfactorily proved, the whole case is proved. It would probably be better if, when the primary condition was satisfied, the court then openly requested evidence on the secondary condition either orally or by way of a written report. It should be the duty of the court to make it clear to the respondent that both issues have been dealt with and proved to the satisfaction of the Justices.

If at the end of the hearing the court cannot decide on the order to be made, it can make an interim order for twenty-eight days in respect of the child. The normal purpose of this is to obtain further information about the child, particularly from the social worker, to enable the court to make a final decision.[3] A request for such an order may also be made by the social worker if he considers that insufficient information on the child is available. It is of course for the court to decide whether to grant the request or not.

As Local Authorities are invariably legally represented in care proceedings, the possibility of the social worker being involved in the cross-examination of witnesses is limited. However, the greater knowledge he has of the child, or of any others giving evidence on the child's behalf, together with all the known factors which have led to the proceedings, the better he can instruct the legal representative in his approach to cross-examination.

For example, if the respondent maintained in his examination-in-chief that he was not beyond the control of his parents or guardian, incidents suggesting that this was untrue, known to the social worker and passed on to the legal representative, could be put to the respondent in order to break down his story. Without the knowledge of such incidents the applicant might find greater difficulty in proving his case. The point to be noted is that the social worker must gather all the available evidence possible to strengthen his case.

The author's present purpose is not to criticise current child legislation, but simply to offer practical guidance on the law as it stands. However, one comment may not be out of place here: the generally low standard of evidence and reports presented to the court may be partly due to the fact that the dice are loaded against the respondent in care proceedings. His ignorance of the proceedings and lack of adequate representation are bound to put him at a disadvantage. Independent representation for the child at all stages of proceedings is well overdue.

The social worker as chief witness in section 2 resolutions

Few social workers are likely to be cast in the role of chief witness in relation to section 2 resolutions, as proceedings arising from the assumption of parental rights by a Local Authority form a minimal part of a

Social Services Department's work. Very often actions which do arise revolve around legal interpretations which are outside the scope of a social worker's duties.

As was noted in Chapter 3, section 2 of the Children Act 1948 (as replaced by section 57 of the Children Act 1975) empowers the Local Authority to assume parental rights over a child in care under section 1 of the Children Act 1948 if certain specific conditions are satisfied. Objection can be made to such assumption, which can lead to court proceedings being initiated by the Local Authority. It has to show the court that its action was justified, otherwise the resolution must lapse.

The specific conditions are in effect a serious reflection on the character, worth and capability of a parent or guardian of a child, which renders him unfit to have care or control of the child. In objecting to the resolution the parent or guardian is therefore challenging the allegation made by the Local Authority. In most cases the resolution has been passed on the recommendation of the social worker who has been involved with the child and his parents. In so far as the Local Authority is concerned, the worker is the person with the greatest knowledge of the case, and will therefore be the Authority's chief witness in the proceedings.

In order to be an effective witness, the social worker must have a sound knowledge of the grounds for passing a resolution. He should be aware that no resolution can be passed unless a child is in care under section 1 of the Children Act 1948, and the condition(s) set out in section 2 of the Act, as substituted by section 57 of the Children Act 1975 can be proved. A recent ruling of five law lords has given power to a Local Authority to assume parental rights over a child while he is in the physical care of the Authority, though this can be challenged by a parent.

The evidence given to the court must show that the material and legal aspects of the resolution have been properly discharged. Thus, if the grounds given were abandonment, it must be proved that the whereabouts of the guardian or parent have remained unknown for not less than twelve months.

The general principles of the perfect witness apply in section 2 resolutions as in other proceedings, but the evidence is specialist in character in that it is confined mainly to one specific condition relating to a parent or guardian. Difficulties can arise from legal complications, but are less likely to do so if careful attention is paid to the specific condition being considered, before a recommendation is made to assume parental rights.

The social worker as advocate

The role of advocate is one which the social worker may be called upon to play where a child who is in the care of a Local Authority has pleaded not guilty to a minor offence, and there is no parent, guardian or legal representative available to act on his behalf. Under such circumstances the social worker, as agent for the Local Authority, would be treated as guardian of the child and given the right to represent him.

There are occasions when the social worker who appears in court with a child should exercise this right, but often he is reluctant to do so, possibly because he is unaware of his rights in court, or because his knowledge of court procedure is too limited.

I use the term *advocate* to describe the protagonist of the defendant. He is *not* engaged to prove the defendant's innocence, as some mistakenly think, but to challenge the prosecutor to prove his guilt. The difference between proving a person's innocence and challenging another to prove his guilt is quite considerable, and any social worker who may be involved in advocacy should be aware of this.

A person may be guilty of an offence and if challenged to prove his innocence would probably find it impossible to do so, yet if another is challenged to prove his guilt this may equally prove to be an impossible task in certain circumstances. As the law stands, the demand is made on the prosecutor not simply to prove guilt, but to prove it beyond reasonable doubt.

As previously stated, the defendant is given a decided but just advantage, and this advantage should be used to the full by his advocate. The advocate must go into battle fully armed with this knowledge and with his course of action clear, whatever his chance of success.

He must follow the evidence of the prosecution with great care, noting possible weaknesses in the evidence given against his client, seeking out discrepancies between one witness and another, uncertainty shown in identification, particular items which leave room for challenge and other matters which he can pursue in cross-examination.

He is then prepared to ask probing questions on the points he has noted with a view to upsetting the evidence given, but should be careful not to labour these. Unless the case is virtually a lost one from the start, there are usually some factors which develop in the course of evidence, and in some instances these may be used to the advantage of the defendant and lead to a 'not guilty' finding.

Hesitancy, for instance, in declaring that the defendant was the person the witness saw, can with skilful questioning lead to an admission that the defendant cannot honestly be identified by the witness. Proof that the witness had a record and was dishonest and completely unreliable could cast doubts on the evidence given. Either of these factors, brought out in cross-examination, may be the first step towards acquittal for the accused

— especially when followed up by further and equally pertinent questions which receive uncertain replies and throw doubt on the testimony.

The attempt to prove innocence is completely unnecessary if the advocate can throw sufficient doubt on the evidence of the prosecution, for if the latter is unable to establish proof beyond reasonable doubt, the case against the defendant *must* be dismissed. The strength of any defence must lie in the ability of the advocate to expose vital weaknesses in the evidence of the prosecution, so it is obvious that every item of evidence must be carefully noted and analysed.

Naturally this is very skilled work, best left in the hands of those trained for it, but on the rare occasions when advocacy is undertaken by the social worker he should have some knowledge of what is entailed. As a professional worker, every social worker involved in the court should have a basic knowledge of the requirements of advocacy.

There is a stronger possibility of the social worker being involved in the work of advocacy in respect of a child in care who has pleaded guilty to an offence. Here, he would present a mitigating plea on behalf of the child. Most frequently this is accomplished by way of a written report to the court, but there is no reason why a plea should not be made orally, even though the court may still request a written report.

This form of advocacy may be undertaken by the social worker and the probation officer in both adult and juvenile courts. A mitigating plea coming from a social worker or probation officer in respect of a person in care or under supervision can, if well presented, be of greater value than one from a legal representative.

The social worker or probation officer as a result of his relationship with so many defendants builds up a greater knowledge and understanding of the offender. In respect of a child or young person he is aware of his needs, his emotions, his growth and development, his attitude to crime, the most suitable method of treatment and many other things about him: this knowledge and understanding enables the social worker or probation officer more readily to make a plea which will assist the court in deciding the most appropriate order.

This of course does not apply to all cases dealt with by social workers and probation officers, but refers specifically to those offenders well known to either service, though as a result of their social enquiries both the social worker and the probation officer can offer specialised help and support to both the juvenile and the adult offender.

It should be pointed out that a plea of mitigation is different from a representation being made to the court in respect of an offender, in which a recommendation is made for custodial measures to be taken. In the latter circumstances it may be argued, particularly in relation to safeguarding the rights of a young person, that with independent representation the recommendation could be challenged. The counter-argument would be that if a custodial measure is under consideration by the court, then the right to legal representation must be offered, even if it is refused or is likely to be refused by the young person.

6. The Social Worker as Reporter

The term *reporter* is here used to indicate the role of the social worker or probation officer in the preparation of reports for or at the request of the court.

In recent years social workers have become very much more involved with court reports, which formerly were mainly undertaken by the probation officer, and frequently they become concerned and anxious about the presentation of reports and the purpose they serve.

Their concern is understandable: although in some circles reports are seen as a valuable asset to the court, there is no set pattern and very few guide-lines available on preparation and presentation.

Writers such as Martin Davies, Andrea Knopf, Peter Ford[1] and others have contributed to the discussion on social enquiry reports, but while their findings offer some interesting and valuable data, they are by no means conclusive and do little more than offer a platform for discussion — some might say argument.

The purpose of the social enquiry report

Some confusion arises from the 'frame of reference' used by each individual reporter in his approach to the preparation and collation of a report. Thus, if he considers the purpose of the report to be the defence of a particular offender, the material he presents will be coloured by this approach. There is no doubt that some reporters do take on the role of advocate when preparing a social enquiry report.

It is not suggested that the following views are free from controversy, but perhaps social work practice is all the healthier for its controversial characteristics. It may be a useful exercise to examine a few 'don'ts' to denote what a report is *not*, before reviewing its purpose and considering how it should be approached and presented.

Don't fall into the trap of thinking that all reports are channels of advocacy on an offender's behalf.

There are some social workers and probation officers who genuinely believe that their purpose in court is to defend the offender at all costs. They probably see the Justices and other participants in the court scene as part of the judicial machinery which must make the offender pay for his misdeeds, and visualising the worst, they take on the role of advocate. Their recommendation becomes a plea for leniency, and so certain facts concerning the offender and his family are either omitted or dressed up in professional jargon, in an effort to persuade the court to 'give the offender another chance'.

It is perfectly in order for any advocate for the defence to use whatever legitimate avenue is open to him, in an attempt to effect an acquittal where there is a plea of not guilty, or to obtain a course of leniency if the offender has pleaded or been found guilty of an offence. He has been engaged for such a purpose, and would be failing in his duty if he did not defend the offender to the limit of his ability. But an enquiry report made at the request of the court should carry no such bias; where it does, this is unlikely to be lost on a sensitive bench, who may treat the whole report as of little value in assisting them to make a proper disposal of a case. The defendant may well be the loser in such circumstances.

Don't be persuaded into thinking that a report is an opportunity for teaching magistrates what social work is all about.

Many harsh criticisms are levelled at the magistrates: some people consider they are far too lenient with hardened young delinquents, while others think they are incompetent, totally incapable of understanding and appreciating the needs of the child, and completely lacking in knowledge on how to deal with him.

I have heard high-ranking social work officers maintaining that one way of teaching magistrates how to do their job is through social enquiry reports. This attitude reveals ignorance of both the magistrate's job and the purpose of a social enquiry report.

Any social worker or probation officer who acts on this principle is likely to be geared to assessment rather than fact as far as a court report is concerned. Any facts presented in the report will be embellished by the reporter's interpretation, and the result will be a social worker's or probation officer's impression rather than a social enquiry. A diagnostic document with planned methods of treatment centred almost entirely upon the offender, and probably with little consideration given to others, is more likely to irritate than instruct the magistrates.

The duty of the magistrate is to judge in accordance with the precepts of the law, and not by the standards of social work, even were these standards beyond criticism. Some social workers maintain that punishment has no part in social work and that therefore it would be quite contrary to their views and conscience to recommend it at any time. However, whether we like it or not, unless our constitution is changed, the law must be respected and obeyed otherwise penalties are incurred. If the law decides that in certain circumstances punishment must be meted out by the magistrates in accordance with statute, they must act accordingly.

There is undoubtedly a great need for consultation and communication between social workers and the magistrates, so that they may appreciate each other's roles and complement each other in the work to be done. The court report which essays to teach the magistrate his duty benefits neither social worker nor magistrate, but can be damaging to the offender.

Don't treat court reports as low in priority.

Recognition must be given to the fact that social workers and probation officers have tremendous commitments, and frequently find it difficult to decide which of their many duties should have priority. Nevertheless, court reports should always be viewed in the light of a high rather than a low priority.

The request for a court report undoubtedly makes a claim on both time and labour, but as specific dates are given for its completion, this does allow for some planning by the worker. The report will assist the court to come to a decision about a juvenile or adult offender, who may be deprived of his freedom for a long period, unless the report can show sound reason why such a course would be inexpedient. The importance of the report is obvious.

From the offender's point of view, a court appearance may have quite a traumatic effect, and the need for support during his trial is apparent. Such support may be better provided after a social enquiry, since through his investigations the social worker is enabled to understand and develop a relationship with the offender, which can benefit the latter both inside and outside the court. The support is strengthened if the worker is able to attend court with the offender.

Care should be taken to ensure that the social enquiry report is before the court on the specified date of hearing, otherwise an adjournment may be necessary. This may annoy the magistrates, but more importantly can add to the distress and concern of the offender.

Social enquiry reports for the Juvenile Court

Section 9(1) of the Children and Young Persons Act 1969 provides specifically that Local Authorities should (unless they consider it unnecessary) provide the court with information relating to the 'home surroundings, school record, health and character of the person in respect of whom the proceedings are brought as it appears to the Authority likely to assist the court' and that the probation service should provide such reports for children of a prescribed age (at present 13 to 16 inclusive).[2] Where either service is already involved with the family it may prepare the court reports on any child of the family.

In some areas the probation service is withdrawing from Juvenile Court proceedings, and frequently in criminal proceedings the Local Authority does not provide reports to the court at the date of the hearing if the child[3] is unknown to them.

In such circumstances, and although reports are available, the court may ask either the Local Authority or the probation officer for reports or further information, and when this request is made the reporters must comply with it.

The request for a social enquiry report by the court normally comes at the end of a case which has been heard. The case must have been proved or the defendant have pleaded guilty in such circumstances.

At this point, a remark which is frequently made by the chairman of the court, especially in relation to a difficult case, is: 'The court would like to know more about you before deciding what should happen, so you will be remanded for two or three weeks for a social worker's or probation officer's report.' The significance of this is then explained to parent and child.

The period of the remand is generally governed by the time considered appropriate by the reporter for him to complete the report, taking into consideration his other commitments. If the remand is on bail the maximum period is four weeks, but if in care (or in custody if young person is deemed unruly) it is limited to three weeks, though further remands can be made if this is considered expedient by the court.

The chairman's remark indicates the purpose of the report: to learn more about the child which will assist in a proper disposal of the case. The reporter should bear this in mind. Thus the emphasis is on the collation of facts concerning the child and his home circumstances, but this by no means precludes an assessment of the facts. If the child is known to the reporter, he is likely to have an awareness of the facts and some understanding of the child and his needs. The more the reporter knows about the child, his background, his environment, etc., and the more aware he is of the child's reactions to certain circumstances, the better he will be able to assist the court.

The reporter should be careful not to use the information he collates for the sole purpose of defending the child against all the odds. The actual information the reporter has is what the court requires, even though this may include an assessment or interpretation of the information.

If the case is new to the reporter, then he has a duty to investigate all the factors affecting the child which can assist the court in the appropriate disposal of the case.

How does the reporter set about his task?

First of all the reporter must remember that he is serving the court. In the Juvenile Court the responsibility is largely that of the social worker in both care and criminal proceedings, though in criminal proceedings the court can request the probation officer to undertake a report on a child from the prescribed age of thirteen to under seventeen. Occasionally this can include a child under thirteen where the family is known to the probation service and the Local Authority approves.

The social worker must also be aware of the fact that he serves the court in the capacity of agent for his employing Authority, who may have to answer for any recommendation he makes. It is no light responsibility and should be taken seriously.

The court has decided on the need for a social enquiry and has entrusted this task to the social worker. As agent for the Local Authority the social worker is under an obligation to prepare the report; this in effect is a statutory duty, and failure to fulfil it could lead to serious repercussions.

The magistrates are under an obligation to judge without bias or prejudice and the social worker or probation officer should approach the preparation of a report in like manner. Care should be taken not to take on the mantle of advocate for the defendant, or teacher to the court, irrespective of the circumstances of the case. The duty of the reporter is to investigate all the circumstances and present his information to the court for final adjudication. In drawing upon the information and knowledge he has of the defendant's needs, he has a right to make a recommendation to the court which may include an unbiased plea for leniency.

Sections 45 and 46 of the Powers of the Criminal Courts Act 1973, should be read in conjunction with this, but put briefly they indicate that no court should pass a sentence of imprisonment or other form of detention before considering a social enquiry report. It appears from this that a court intending to deliver a custodial sentence may be led by a report to consider other alternatives. Primarily a social enquiry report is requested with a view to assisting the court in determining the most suitable method of dealing with any person in respect of an offence (section 46). Thus in very many cases a well prepared report has assisted the court in taking action which has benefited the offender without depriving him of his liberty. If a report can indeed assist both court and offender, care in its preparation is obviously essential.

In setting about the task of preparing a report the reporter must decide what information is necessary and how this can best be collated. In some cases the court may set the 'terms of reference' by deciding specific matters to be investigated. For instance, if there is doubt about the physical or mental health of the defendant, there may be a request for medical and psychiatric reports, which the reporter may arrange to have completed, and submitted to the court together with his own. Should there be some question about where the defendant has been residing it would be the reporter's duty to investigate the situation.

Generally, the collation of the report is left to the reporter, and the court's main concern is that it should be completed in time and offer satisfactory assistance in disposing of the case in the most appropriate manner.

Some lawyers have strong feelings over the apparent power vested in the reporter in the preparation of social enquiry reports. They feel that he has too much freedom in the collation of his information, too many sources he can tap for views and observations (particularly on a child) which may be incorporated in the report, but which are not based on the reporter's actual knowledge of the child and the family background. They believe that such second-hand information may be detrimental to the parents or child, but despite this the reporter can still make use of it in a report. The view is not without justification.

Against this it may be argued that a social enquiry report is not used to prove guilt or otherwise, but to give a background picture of the child which perhaps may assist the court in reaching its final decision. To obtain the background data it is essential to tap all sources of information, and carefully assess the 'second-hand' items for reliability, etc. Anything which has come from another source, or is hearsay in character, should be made clear in the report and should corroborate the reporter's own findings.

Probably the problem does not lie so much in the power invested in the reporter in the Juvenile Court as in the weakness of the system. Reports are open to questioning but are too rarely questioned, either because the representative has had too little time to study the report which he normally only receives at the time of the hearing.

This strengthens the argument for independent representation and the right of a representative to have copies of evidence and reports in advance of the hearing date. A closer examination of reports by representatives may lead to more balanced judgements being made.

There is also a suggestion made by many that the reporter should simply report facts and leave the rest to the court. Those who think thus believe that the reporter should have no right to make a recommendation on the final disposal of a case. The Lord Chief Justice has quashed this view, and probably rightly so. The reporter has investigated all the circumstances and noted all that is going on within an individual or family, emotionally, physically and mentally; were he then to confine himself to plain facts, it is doubtful whether the court could be assisted in reaching its final decision.

All his observations must lead the reporter to some personal assessment of the situation, and this is part of the information required by the court. The court may be influenced but is not bound by a reporter's recommendation or assessment: if neither appears to tally with the facts in the report then it would be a weak bench which would accept them.

It is essential, of course, in presenting facts in a report, to ensure that these can be substantiated. For example, it may be clearly seen by the reporter that a certain child is beyond the control of his parents, but not that he is violent as stated by them. Under such circumstances it would be acceptable to say that he was beyond control (outlining known incidents to substantiate this), but not to add that he was violent. Should there be a need to introduce the latter idea then it would be advisable to state, 'According to his parents he is violent.' In this way the reporter suggests to the court that he has no personal knowledge of the violence, but that the parents could substantiate this if they were called upon to do so.

Great care should be taken in differentiating between fact and impression. In most interviews we form impressions of the other person, and these can readily lead to opinions which are then stated as facts. This is a common and dangerous practice which should be avoided. A fact *is*, an impression is *what we think it is*. Thus, 'I don't like the appearance of that person' soon becomes 'He is a villain.' The point need not be laboured, but it might be worth while noting that *impressions* appear as *facts* more frequently than is imagined in court reports.

Much the same applies to glib comments, such as 'He comes from a good home', which has no significance since nothing is said about the home to enable the court to form its own opinion; similarly, 'His parents say he is a good boy' when he is appearing in court for the third or fourth time. Fatuous remarks of this nature do nothing at all to assist the court in determining the most suitable method of dealing with the child.

Since the young offender in the Juvenile Court is a child who normally resides with his parents or guardian and is maintained by them, it is clear that the home should be visited and the parents or guardian interviewed as well as the offender. On a factual basis, it is the parents or guardian who can give information about when and where the child was born, any important features regarding his birth and development, and any serious illness or incident which may have affected him. They can discuss his school, attendance, behaviour and progress there, which can then be compared with any school report prepared by the Education Authority for the court. If they have experienced any problem with him, they can discuss this and indicate how it affects himself and the family, and state when the problem was first noticed. Problems seen by one parent may be viewed quite differently by the other, and the reason for this should be elicited and assessed by the reporter.

Indeed, part of the reporter's function is to draw out as much information as possible from the parents, and analyse it with care and skill as much for his own benefit as for that of the court, particularly if there is a strong possibility that the child will come under his supervision as a result of the court hearing. The report, therefore, has two advantages; firstly, it yields considerable information from which the reporter may gain ideas for possible forms of treatment, and secondly, when properly prepared and presented it is of assistance to the court in reaching its decision. In particular, the parents' attitude to the child and his to them, together with the interactions going on within the family, may be noted and form a good platform upon which the reporter can build.

Individual interviews

Because of the dual value of the social enquiry report, as stated above, much depends upon the manner in which the reporter sets about his task, and how painstaking he is in gathering information surrounding all the circumstances. It is very common for parents and other members of the family to form a united front against an outsider who has to make enquiries about another member, although there may in fact be considerable discord within the home.

It is certainly no uncommon feature for one parent to have reservations about saying too much in the presence of the other parent. Experience may have taught them that this leads to further friction between them, when their marriage relationship is none too stable. This can undoubtedly limit the information likely to be forthcoming, and lead to vital factors being omitted or glossed over. To work with such limited information is unlikely to be in the best interests of the child.

Therefore, although it is important to see the parents and family together where possible, to gain some impression of the family dynamics, and the interactions between one member of the unit and another, nevertheless it is advisable also to see the parents and child individually. This may be time-consuming but the end result will be more profitable. A mother, father or child may speak more openly, truthfully and sincerely in a one-to-one interview than in a collective discussion, and the result may offer a more accurate assessment of the family background.

In the course of a home visit it is important to be observant, and though the reporter should be a good listener he should also be a good observer. On occasion, what the eyes see can throw doubt on what the ears hear. For example, a father who was out of work for a lengthy period stoutly maintained that he was not a lazy man, offering all manner of excuses for his inability to find employment. At the same time the reporter noted that cupboard doors were hanging loosely on their hinges for the want of a few screws. This, together with other small items, raised doubts about the father's attitude towards his home and family, which in later interviews were confirmed, leading to a more accurate assessment of the family situation.

When there is some divergence in the information gathered, it is advisable not to hazard a guess but rather to expend a little more effort, and if necessary go over some of the ground again as this may help to establish the facts. Additionally, it is helpful to verify the information from other appropriate sources if this is possible.

In addition to seeing the child in the family setting, one should also remember that he has a place in the community and at school. The reporter should therefore learn something about the community in which he lives: if he attends a club or organisation what part does he play? How is he seen by the club leader and club members? Who are his associates and what is his status with them — leader or led? The answers to these and similar questions help to develop a composite picture of the child, his family and his surroundings, which can lead to a more accurate assessment of his character, personality and needs.

Information concerning his school life should be obtained from the school he attends (although it is general practice for the court to request a school report, and if this can be seen by the reporter before he makes his final recommendation, it may be helpful).

After all the information has been gathered it is then necessary to edit a report for the court. As stated earlier, there is no set pattern laid down for this, although most Authorities may offer guide-lines for the worker, nevertheless the manner of presenting the report is his own.

The presentation of the report

Without drawing up a prototype report, it is suggested that the following points should be covered in a social enquiry for the magistrates.

(a)   An outline of the family. This should include the composition of the family together with the income of each working member of the family (particularly the earnings of the parents) and of the subject of the report if he is working or earning money in any way. The relationships existing between parents, parents and other members of the family and child himself are important: include sibling relationships and relationships with close relatives where appropriate. Strengths and weaknesses within the family should be carefully noted with special emphasis on those which affect the child.

(b) Details of the home. In this respect, note should be taken whether the home is owned or rented, the mortgage or rental payments and whether there are any arrears, and the area in which the home is situated. The standard of comfort and cleanliness and the atmosphere which prevails all help in the development of the assessment.

(c) The antecedents of the child. This is a very important item in a social enquiry report and one which the court must consider carefully before deciding upon any course of action. A statutory duty is imposed upon the court to be informed of any offender's antecedents and though this information may be given by the police, it is often presented by the reporter whose investigations should ensure its accuracy as far as is possible.

Antecedents include records of any illnesses suffered by the child or any member of the family which may have affected him, previous offences with the methods of treatment ordered, together with the effects of the treatment, and also the child's attitude to the current offence or complaint. An assessment can be made of whether this appears to be an isolated incident or one which is likely to be repeated. Some indication should also be given of interests, hobbies, work, general behaviour and attitudes which may have some bearing on the final decision of the court.

(d) Facts about and a brief assessment of the child. All relevant information concerning or affecting the child should be gathered together to give as full a picture as possible of the *whole child*, and not just carefully selected parts. The facts should be capable of substantiation, and are to be used to make an assessment of the child's needs: this is important for the ultimate recommendation made to the court. It is in this particular area that the reporter may be tempted to present the strengths of the person and omit the weaknesses, especially when it is felt that the report is intended as a defence.

(e) Information concerning the school record. In most cases the court will have reports from the Head of the school or appropriate Education Authority. However, the quality of these can vary quite considerably, so any additional information which can be obtained may be of great value to the court and the child. The reporter should endeavour to find out how many schools have been attended, the record of the child in

each, the regularity of attendance, the child's attitude to school work, his attainments and his behaviour. Where there are differences between one school and another, some indication should be given of the cause of these. A good relationship built up between the school and the reporter can undoubtedly help in the assessment of the child.

(f)   A short case work assessment. It has been said that the reporter should not use a social enquiry report as a channel for teaching the court the elements of social work, but it would be impossible for him to offer effective help to the magistrates without any assessment of the character and characteristics of the child, together with some indication of his needs. The reporter has seen much more than the bare facts of the case, and this knowledge can only be embodied in an assessment of the situation. However, the assessment should have considerable bearing on the facts presented (otherwise it may be dismissed as valueless by the court), and it should be as brief as possible, though sufficient to indicate to the magistrates the needs of the child.

(g)   Conclusion. This should be a relatively short summing-up of all the main factors in the report, and should lead to a recommendation.

(h)   Recommendation. This is probably the most important aspect of the report to the reporter, but not necessarily to the court, which may have other reports to consider. The reporter is naturally hoping that his recommendation will be accepted, otherwise he feels his efforts have been wasted. The court, on the other hand, must consider the circumstances of the case, the nature of the offence and any other reports, and its final decision may be quite opposed to the recommendation made in the social enquiry report.

Care should be taken, therefore, to ensure that the recommendation follows on naturally from the observations made in the body of the report. No recommendation divorced from the substance of the report is likely to influence the magistrates. It has been known for reporters to paint a rather damning picture of an individual and then conclude with a recommendation for a conditional discharge. Such a recommendation can hardly be expected to carry much authority.

The recommendation in a report may usefully include some reference to the likely outcome of different kinds of disposal, but such reference cannot or should not be made without some knowledge of the methods of disposal open to the court. The orders available, together with their purpose, significance and effectiveness are too extensive to cover in this short manual, but the reporter is advised to acquaint himself with them for the purpose of preparing social enquiry reports.[4]

There are some writers who disagree strongly with the views expressed above, and Phillip Bean in an excellent article entitled 'The Challenge of Social Enquiry Reports', published in *Family Law* (January/February 1974), has some very critical remarks to make about probation officers and social workers.

He considers that social workers feel free to make recommendations in spite of their ignorance of the courts, sentencing and penal institutions. His comments may be open to argument but they are not without some merit, and should be considered seriously both by social workers and probation officers.

A comment in *The Magistrate*, March 1973 is unlikely to be well received by those whose views correspond with Phillip Bean's, but it does state the current position of social enquiry reports.

Magistrates have been heard to say that if a probation officer or social worker includes in a social enquiry report recommendation as to the disposal of a case he is exceeding his authority and usurping the functions of the court. This view is not held by Lord Widgery, The Lord Chief Justice.

He recently gave authority to the editor of this journal to quote him as having said that if an experienced officer feels able to make a specific recommendation in favour of or against any particular form of decision being reached, he should state it clearly in his report.

The recommendation may for example be for, or against, a period of supervision or a custodial sentence; it may commend the view that a monetary penalty would have a salutory effect; if a scheme were available in the locality that a community service order or a day training requirement should be considered; or simply that a medical report should be sought.

Before reaching a decision magistrates receive information from several sources and there will undoubtedly be cases in which the court will find itself unable to accept the officer's recommendation. They will make the decision they think appropriate. That is the court's right — and its duty.

We hope probation officers and social workers whose duty it is to prepare and present reports to the court will be encouraged by the benches they serve to make recommendations in precise terms when appropriate.

It should be added to this that probation officers and social workers ought also to be encouraged to learn more about the methods of treatment and punishment at present available, so their recommendation of a particular course is made with knowledge and experience, and is therefore worthy of consideration. This applies to recommendations made in all courts.

Social enquiry reports for the Magistrates' Court

Some thought should be given to the fact that social enquiry reports prepared at the request of the Magistrates' Court differ in some respects in approach and substance from those prepared for the Juvenile Court.

Social workers in particular must appreciate that the welfare of the offender is not the first consideration (except in the case of a juvenile appearing with an adult) in a Magistrates' Court. As has been stated elsewhere: 'The courts are not welfare agencies; their principal function in sentencing is the preservation of law and order. They have no special knowledge of moral questions or whether one way of life, however eccentric or even repugnant to the bench, is any more or less socially desirable than another, provided only that it does not involve transgressing the criminal law. Once the bench have assisted an offender towards a law-abiding way of life their rehabilitative function is discharged.'[5]

There are cases, of course, where the court is very much interested in the welfare of an offender, especially when it is obvious that the needs of the person far outweigh the gravity of the offence. In such cases the general principles of sentencing may be overlooked in an effort to help the individual.

In most cases the welfare of the offender is linked with the need to avoid a repetition of the offence. It would be wrong to suggest that the reporter should not place emphasis on the welfare of the offender, whom he may be called upon to supervise, but nevertheless he must be aware of the function of the court. Overemphasis of the offender's welfare, to the exclusion of the nature of his offence and other circumstances, is unlikely to be accepted by the court.

Thus the reporter's approach should be to satisfy the court's requirements. The welfare of the offender should be met within the courses open to the magistrates and this again demands both knowledge and experience on the part of the reporter of the methods of disposal available.

The substance of a social enquiry report in a Magistrates' Court could be said to be geared to the individual rather than to the family, as in the Juvenile Court. In a Magistrates' Court, or higher court, the offender stands very much on his own, and the family circumstances, though frequently taken into account, do not so readily affect the disposal of a case.

Relating to this, it must be accepted that access to the family background may not be available. The offender, as an adult, is considered to be a responsible person in his own right. He can refuse to give details of his family, and demand that they are not made aware of the offence. With regard to a report he is in effect master of his own destiny.

The reporter must be aware of this and thus draw out all the information he can with considerable tact and skill. If some information on the family background can be collated, this is good, especially in the case of a young offender, but it need not be stressed as in a report to the Juvenile Court. Home circumstances are important, however, and should be noted carefully where possible.

Where no set pattern is imposed, the reporter is left to develop his own style of report presentation. However, the following factors should be considered, investigated where possible and included in the report:

(a)   the offender's background,
(b)   previous offences, methods of treatment and responses,
(c)   present offence,
(d)   attitude to offence,
(e)   school or work record,
(f)   associates and their mutual influences,
(g)   relationships with others, and how they affect the offender,
(h)   interests and hobbies and how they may be utilised to his benefit,
(i)   responses to varying situations (as, for example, his reaction to failure, disappointment and frustration, or to success, acceptance, etc.: this can often indicate the appropriate type of treatment),
(j)   strengths and weaknesses,
(k)   possible response to supervision and other forms of treatment.

One final comment should be made with reference to pre-trial reports. Some courts prefer to have reports available at the conclusion of a case, irrespective of whether there has been a plea of guilty or not guilty. An advantage in this is that adjournments for the preparation of reports by social worker or probation officer are minimised.

Pre-trial reports are not viewed with favour by the probation service and they do have their disadvantages, particularly in the area where the defendant is unknown to the reporter. In the first instance, if there is a plea of not guilty, a report should not be undertaken without the consent of the defendant, even though the court is presumed not to see the report except when there is a finding of guilty. The preparation of a pre-trial report can suggest that there may be a pre-judgement of the case, though this is not necessarily so. But if a recommendation has to be made, it can only be based on the assumption that the defendant is guilty, and it is open to question how much this may colour a report, or the approach to one. It may also be queried whether the information given to the reporter might have differed if given after the hearing, when the court had decided the guilt of the defendant.

Though the approach to a pre-trial social enquiry report may differ from that to a normal report, the information to be gathered is similar and requires no reiteration.

7. Reports in Guardianship, Matrimonial and Custodianship Proceedings

Reports requested under these proceedings differ quite substantially from social enquiry reports and can be more accurately called welfare reports. In general they are prepared by court welfare officers when proceedings are heard in the High Court, and by the probation officer when the hearings are in the County Court or Magistrates' Court.

The reporter should note that while his report centres around the child's welfare, as does the social enquiry report, the vital facts to be elicited focus mainly on the parents or applicants in any hearing. He should be able to approach his task more objectively, however, since he is less likely mistakenly to consider its purpose as protecting the child from the judiciary.

Guardianship of minors

In relation to an applicant for custody under section 9 of the Guardianship of Minors Act 1971, the court may request a report from a probation officer or social worker on *matters relevant to the application*. (See section 6(1) of the Guardianship Act 1973.) The court will specify these matters and the reporter is under an obligation to investigate and report upon them either orally or in writing.

The specific matter may be important but relatively limited, such as an investigation into the means of one or both of the parties; or it may entail a more thorough enquiry into the suitability of the applicants. The former matter may be speedily completed, but the latter will require more investigation into the home circumstances, the character and life-style of the applicants, the relationship with the child and how this is reciprocated, and the provision which can be made for the proper care and maintenance of the child. Although in many cases this kind of investigation requires considerable care, patience and skill, it does have the advantage that the specific requirements of the court are known to the reporter.

Under the Guardianship Acts the court has power in exceptional circumstances to make a supervision order at the same time as a custody order, and if it considers it expedient may make an order committing the child to the care of a Local Authority. The same will apply when custodianship proceedings under the Children Act 1975 are brought into operation. In the course of his investigations the reporter may discover strong grounds for considering such orders and his findings should be incorporated in the report to the court.

Formerly, in accordance with section 6 of the Guardianship Act 1973, it was necessary for the written reports to be read aloud to the court, to ascertain if there was any matter which either party or his representative wished to call in question. If so, the reporter had to give evidence on the matter raised, and the party or his representative had the right to call witnesses to refute this. This ruling has been amended by section 90 of the Children Act 1975, and it is now at the discretion of the court whether the written report or part of it is read aloud. A copy of the report, however, must be given to each party or his legal representative either before or during the hearing of the application. Also the court itself, either party or his legal representative may call the reporter to give evidence on any disputed factor in the report. The party or representative can then give or call evidence to refute the evidence of the reporter.

A single Justice can request a report before the hearing of an application, and this report would be made on behalf of the court hearing the case.

Committal to care

Where the court proposes to make an order committing a child to care, the appropriate Authority must be given an opportunity of making representation to the court, particularly with regard to the financial provision to be made for the child.

Exceptional circumstances must prevail before the court can take such action, and there must be strong grounds for the belief that it is impracticable or undesirable for the child to be entrusted to the care of either parent or to an independent person. Although the representation may be made by the legal section of the Local Authority, the task of investigating the matter and preparing a report is that of the social worker.

Exhaustive enquiries should be carried out for such a report to establish the circumstances of either party, or of any independent person who might be involved. It may prove possible to collect facts which will cause the court to reconsider its proposal, but these must be very convincing to affect the final decision. It should be clearly understood that making such a representation does not mean that the Local Authority can refuse a committal to care. It simply means the Authority must be given the opportunity to show good reason why a care order may be inappropriate, or to ensure that satisfactory financial provision is made for the child.

The Matrimonial Proceedings (Magistrates' Courts) Act 1960

This Act is still in operation at the time of writing but the Domestic Proceedings and Magistrates' Courts Act 1978 will gradually supersede it. Both Acts are therefore included in this book.

Under the Matrimonial Proceedings (Magistrates' Courts) Act 1960, the court can request an oral or written report from a probation officer or officer of a Local Authority on specific matters relating to a decision the court has to make. Such a request is made when the court has insufficient information on the following matters which have to be decided:

(a)   Any complaints under section 1 of the Act which includes desertion, persistent cruelty, being found guilty on indictment to assault on complainant, etc., adultery, drunkenness or drug addiction, having intercourse with complainant while knowingly suffering from venereal disease (without the complainant's knowledge), compelling wife to submit to prostitution, wilful neglect by husband to maintain wife and family, and wilful neglect by wife to provide for husband under certain circumstances.

(b)   Variation of a matrimonial order, and

(c)   Revocation of a matrimonial order.

It can be seen from this that there is a wide range of factors which may lead to a request for a report, but the scope of the report itself is narrowed to a specific subject.

This illustrates the difference between a social enquiry report and a welfare report as requested by the courts. The one satisfying feature, however, is that the reporter knows exactly what enquiry he has to make although he may have difficulty on occasions in limiting the amount of information he gathers to satisfy the requirements of the court. Probably the wisest principle here is to keep as close as possible to the requirements of the court. In asking for a report on a specific point the court has indicated that it has insufficient information on that particular matter to reach a final decision.

Section 4 of the Matrimonial Proceedings Act has been amended by section 91 of the Children Act 1975, which brings it into line with section 6 of the Guardianship Act 1973 as amended by section 90 of the Children Act 1975.

This gives the court discretion on whether to read a written report or part of it in open court. Copies of the report must be given to the parties or their legal representatives either before or during the hearing of the complaint. The reporter can be called to give evidence on matters raised in the report by the court, or at the request of the parties or representatives, who in turn can themselves give evidence or call evidence in relation to the matter raised. It would appear that a single Justice cannot request a report under this section.

The Act enables a court to make a supervision order with a matrimonial order where exceptional circumstances exist. An order committing a child to the care of a Local Authority is also within the power of the court, where there are exceptional circumstances and the court is of the opinion that it would be impracticable or undesirable for a child to be entrusted to either parent or to an independent person.

If the court proposes to commit the child to care the court must notify the Local Authority of its intention within ten days, and the Authority has the right to make representation. The procedure is similar to that under the Guardianship Acts.

Possibly the most difficult type of report the reporter will have to prepare is when a decision has to be made between two parents, or between parents and another applicant, for the custody of a child. The weighing up of the situation may be no easy task even to the best legal minds, and the reporter may tend to lose sight of the legalities and be more concerned with emotional aspects of the situation. Where the merits of the parties appear to be evenly balanced the difficulty in recommendation is obvious.

This type of report should be prepared by a very experienced officer, who is aware of the pitfalls and is able to assess a situation with accuracy, impartiality but with considerable feeling. A clinical approach should be avoided and the testing of theories treated with care.

Domestic Proceedings and Magistrates' Courts Act 1978

This Act repeals the Matrimonial Proceedings (Magistrates' Courts) Act 1960 and brings domestic proceedings in the Magistrates' Court into line with other Acts.

The grounds for application for a matrimonial order are contained in section 1 of the Act and are applicable to either party of the marriage. The grounds are that the respondent

(a)　has failed to provide reasonable maintenance for the applicant,

(b)　has failed to provide, or to make a proper contribution towards reasonable maintenance for any child of the family,

(c)　has behaved in such a way that the applicant cannot reasonably be expected to live with the respondent, or

(d)　has deserted the applicant.

Before the court can dismiss or make a final order on an application made on any of these grounds it must consider any child or children of the marriage who may be under the age of eighteen (see section 8(1).) In this respect it has power to make an order regarding custody and access. (See section 8 (2) (a) (b).) If an order for custody is made, this may be linked with a supervision order where there are exceptional circumstances warranting such an action (section 9), and similarly where there are exceptional circumstances which make it impractical or undesirable for the child to be entrusted to either parent or any other individual, then the court can commit the child to care (section 10).

If the court is of the opinion that it has insufficient information to decide on a course of action under sections 8 to 10, then a request may be made to a local authority social worker or probation officer to furnish an oral or written report on specified matters (section 12).

The procedure for making a representation as to committal to care is similar to that in guardianship proceedings. The court may request the reporter to give evidence on any matter contained in any report made by him, and must request him to do so if this is required by either party or their representatives. Evidence can then be called to attempt to refute the evidence of the reporter.

Section 14 of the Act gives power to the court to grant access to a grandparent of a child, and as section 12 applies to this, it seems that the magistrates can request a social worker or probation officer to furnish a report on matters relating to the grandparent.

The same applies to the variation or revocation of an order as in section 21(5), and in this respect the probation officer can apply for such a variation or revocation if he is supervising the family, as also can a social worker, who in addition can make similar applications in respect of a child in the care of his Authority.

Where a report relates to reconciliation (discussed in Chapte 9), nothing said by either party to the marriage to or in the presence of the reporter should be contained in the report unless both parties have consented to its inclusion. If it is included without consent it cannot be accepted as evidence.

Though primarily intended to bring matrimonial proceedings in the Magistrates' Courts into line with those in other courts, the 1978 Act effects other changes which deserve comment.

It will still be possible for stipendiary magistrates in London and other metropolitan areas to hear domestic proceedings alone, but the appointment of Justices for the Domestic Court will be limited to those specially selected as members of a Domestic Court Panel. This should ensure greater specialisation and, hopefully, more effective results in the court.

In relation to social workers, it is obvious that their duties must increase in the Domestic Court, which will become the venue of adoption and custodianship proceedings. Therefore they may well become more involved in guardianship matters.

Family Law Reform Act 1969

If a ward of court is committed to the care of a Local Authority in accordance with the provisions of the Family Law Reform Act 1969, section 7, there is no right of representation by the Local Authority. These proceedings are heard in the High Court, which has a right to direct the Local Authority as to the maintenance and treatment of a ward of court.

Matrimonial Causes Act 1973

Under section 43 of the Matrimonial Causes Act 1973, the High Court or County Court has power to commit a child to care where there are exceptional circumstances making it impracticable or undesirable for the child to be entrusted to either parent or to any independent person. In this case the Local Authority has a right to make representation to the court and the social worker may be involved in investigations to help his employing Authority in the matter.

Reports in custodianship proceedings

Custodianship is a new concept in child legislation, introduced by the Children Act 1975, which has yet to be implemented.

The idea springs from the Houghton Report and caters for persons who, though not the natural parents, have been or will be responsible for the long-term care of a child. Such persons (for example foster parents) have no legal status or rights over the child: the only way to obtain this is through adoption, which severs the links with the child's natural family.

Custodianship has therefore been introduced to offer legal security to foster parents, etc., by giving them a limited form of legal custody while retaining the child's links with its natural parents. As we shall see, it is not available for parents and certain other persons who have other means of obtaining custody of a child.

What is a custodianship order?

A custodianship order can be made by an authorised court on the application of a qualified person, and when made it vests in that person legal custody of the child. There is some confusion about what powers and responsibilities reside in the custodian under the terms 'legal custody'.

Section 86 of the Act states: 'In this Act, unless the context requires otherwise, *legal custody* means, as respect a child, so much of the parental rights and duties as relate to the person of the child (including the place and manner in which his time is spent); but a person shall not by virtue of having legal custody of the child be entitled to effect or arrange for his emigration from the United Kingdom unless he is a parent or guardian of the child.'

Matters concerning a child's person include the right to determine his education, his need for medical treatment, the manner in which his development should be fostered, the place where he resides and how he behaves. The right to effect or arrange emigration apparently still remains with the parent or guardian, as do all matters relating to any property which is or might become the child's. Schedule 3 (7) indicates that a custodian's consent to marriage is necessary, but he cannot give agreement to adoption or determine the child's nationality or domicile.

The order for custodianship is subject to revocation or variation on the application of a parent, guardian or other specified person.

Who may apply for a custodianship order?

Any person (with the exception of the mother or father of the child and in specified cases the step-parent) can apply for the order but there are qualifications which should be noted.

Should a relative or qualified step-parent make the application, this must be with the consent of the person who has legal custody, and the child must have had its home with the applicant for the three months immediately preceding the application. A step-parent is not qualified to make an application for an order if the child has been named in an order making arrangements for the welfare of the children of the family in divorce proceedings under section 41 (1) of the Matrimonial Causes Act 1973.

Any other person making an application for a custodianship order must have the consent of the person who has legal custody, and the child must have had his home with the applicant for a period or periods amounting to twelve months including the three months preceding the application.

In a situation where a child has had his home with any person for a period or periods amounting to three years before the application is made, that person can apply for a custodianship order without the consent of the person having legal custody. The latter can of course contest the issue if he so desires.

If no one has legal custody of the child, if the applicant himself has legal custody, or if the person having legal custody cannot be found, then a relative or qualified step-parent of the child can apply for an order without consent of the person having legal custody, if the child has had his home with the relative for three months preceding the application. Alternatively, any other person can apply for an order without consent being necessary, if the child has had his home with that person for a period or periods amounting to twelve months including the three months prior to the application.

It may be seen that the scope for obtaining custody of a child in one form or another will widen perceptibly when custodianship legislation is implemented. The proceedings will be very much governed by the principles of the Guardianship Acts, but have some affinity with adoption proceedings.

The contents of reports

Social workers will be very much involved in custodianship proceedings in the capacity of reporters. Their role will have a dual characteristic; one in which the social worker will be solely responsible by statute, the other in which either he or the probation officer may be involved at the request of the court. In relation to the statutory report, when any person makes an application for a custodianship order he has to notify the Local Authority within seven days, unless the Authority or the court extends this period. On receipt of the applicant's notice, the Authority *must* appoint an officer (social worker) to make a report to the court on prescribed matters and including any other matter he considers relevant to the application.

The prescribed matters will be set out in regulations drawn up by the Secretary of State; while these have not yet been established, they will include the following.

(a) The wishes and feelings of the child. These are considered taking into account his age and understanding and all other matters relevant to the operation of section 1 (the principle on which questions relating to custody are decided) of the Guardianship of Minors Act 1971. This section places the welfare of the child as the most important consideration, before any claim of one parent over another.

(b) The means and suitability of the applicant. The investigation in this respect would appear to be similar to that undertaken when dealing with an applicant for adoption. It may well be that in some cases the original application was for an adoption order and as a result of that investigation into means and suitability it has been shown that the application would be more appropriate as an application for custodianship.

(c) Information of a kind specified in the regulations relating to members

of the applicant's household. Unless he is with a relative, the child who is in the actual custody of an applicant pending the result of the application will be a protected child, and the reporter will need to investigate all members of the household to ensure there is no one residing there who is debarred by statute from having contact with a child under these circumstances.

(d)   The wishes and the means of the mother and father of the child. A custodianship order, unlike an adoption order, is not irrevocable, so either parent may by order of the court have to make a contribution to the custodian for the maintenance of the child. It appears from section 34 of the Children Act 1975, that the custodian must make an application for such contribution, and it may thus be necessary for the reporter to learn whether the custodian intends to do so.

When the regulations are eventually drawn up the work of the reporter may bear a marked similarity to the role of guardian *ad litem* in adoption proceedings.

The report which is requested by the court is rather closer to that involved in Guardianship and Matrimonial Proceedings, in that it must contain certain specified matters, in accordance with sections 36 and 39 of the Children Act 1975. Section 36 places a duty on the court to ascertain who would have legal custody of a child before a custodianship order is revoked. If no person has legal custody, the court shall commit the child to the care of the appropriate Local Authority if it decides to revoke the order. This may occur in situations where it is the custodian who applies for the revocation of the order and there is no person with legal custody to whom the child can be returned.

In other circumstances, although there is someone who would have legal custody if the order were revoked, the court may commit the child to care because it considers it undesirable for that person to have custody of the child. Alternatively the court may allow the person to have custody but at the same time make a supervision order in the interests of the child.

Before making any of these decisions, however, the court must request a local authority officer or probation officer to furnish a report (unless sufficient information is already available), and the officer must comply with the court's request. These reports are governed by section 2 (2) to (6) of the Guardianship Act 1973 and have been outlined earlier. They may be made orally or in writing.

Under section 39, the court in dealing with any application in relation to custodianship proceedings may request a local authority officer or probation officer to furnish a report on any specified matter, and again the officer must comply with the request. These reports too are governed by section 2 (2) to (6) of the Guardianship Act 1973 as amended by the Children Act 1975, section 90.

It is clear that the social worker will become very much more involved in the work of the Domestic Court in relation to custodianship proceedings, and it would be well for him to prepare himself for this by looking closely at the role he is likely to play in this setting.

8. The Role of Guardian *ad litem*

Formerly the appointment of guardian *ad litem* was only made by the court in adoption proceedings, but since 26 November 1976 this has been extended to cover applications for the discharge or variation of supervision or care orders made in care proceedings which are unopposed. At a later date they will be further extended to include all care and related proceedings, but not custodianship proceedings.

The courts make the appointments from a special panel of persons who have been nominated for the purpose and these include probation officers, social workers and other suitable individuals. Nominations for these appointments are made by Directors of Social Services, Chief Probation Officers and similar responsible people.

The DHSS circular LAC (76) 20 states:

> Persons required to undertake guardian *ad litem* duties should have practical experience of social work with families and children under stress, as well as with children needing to live temporarily or permanently apart from their parents. The ability to communicate effectively with children of all ages is of primary importance in the selection of persons to act as guardian *ad litem*. Bearing in mind that guardians *ad litem* will be required to examine social work records and will need to have the status necessary to give their social work colleagues and courts confidence in their advice, they should normally be experienced social workers and probation officers. Ideally they should be people with professional casework training plus relevant post work training experience. Experience of court work in care and related proceedings will be especially important.
>
> Guardians *ad litem* can also be appointed on a part-time basis, and former probation officers and social workers who have retired may well be very suitable and valuable appointments.

It may be seen from this that care must be taken in the selection of these appointments, and also that the extension of guardian *ad litem* appointments to all care and related proceedings makes the guardian *ad litem* very much a part of the court setting. Many social workers and probation officers will be appointed in this capacity, and they should be aware of their duties.[1]

The guardian *ad litem* in adoption proceedings

Before contemplating the role of guardian *ad litem* in care proceedings, it is convenient to examine this role in the more traditional field of adoption.

In relation to adoption, the role often follows that of the adoption welfare officer, though this is not necessarily so, and certainly not where his Local Authority has placed a child for adoption. Under the latter circumstances the appropriate officer of the Local Authority (the Director of Social Services) cannot be appointed as guardian *ad litem*.[2]

Adoption welfare begins when the applicants take over the care of a child below school-leaving age, provided they are not parents, guardians or relatives of the child, or when notice of intention to adopt is received by the Local Authority. The child then becomes a protected child.

The duty of the adoption welfare officer (social worker) is to safeguard the interests of the child, a function which is taken over by the guardian *ad litem* when he is appointed by the court.

The duties of the guardian *ad litem*, who effectively is working under the instructions of the court to which he is responsible, are laid down in the Adoption (County Court) Rules 1976 and the Magistrates' Courts (Adoption) Rules 1976. Normally the Official Solicitor is requested to act as guardian *ad litem* in applications made to the High Court and his appointment is governed by the Adoption (High Court) Rules 1976. As the social worker is unlikely to be involved in the High Court proceedings these will not be examined here.

As stated, the main function of the guardian *ad litem* is to safeguard the interests of the child; he will investigate as far as possible all the circumstances of the proposed adoption, and will then prepare a written report for the court. This report is a confidential document. Throughout his investigations he has free access to the court and may receive its direction on any matter. Under certain circumstances he may be requested to complete an interim report, but the occasions for this are rare.

When the guardian *ad litem* is appointed he will receive from the court all the necessary documents which enable him to make his investigation. These documents include the application for the adoption order, duly completed by the applicants, their medical certificates, their marriage certificate, the mother's or other person's agreement to adoption, the child's medical form and birth certificate, and information about all those who are respondents in the case.

Every document must be thoroughly checked by the guardian *ad litem*, and where endorsements are necessary (as in the mother's agreement and child's birth certificate) he must ensure that these have been effected. He must verify with the applicants that everything stated in their application form is correct, and satisfy himself as far as this is possible that this is so.

Interviews: the applicants

He is required to interview every applicant and ascertain from each why they wish to adopt the child. This entails looking carefully at the motivation of the applicants, and where this involves a married couple, noting whether one has a greater motivation than the other, and what effect this may have if an adoption order is made.

It is always advisable to reiterate the significance of adoption, that it vests the parental rights and duties relating to the child in the adopters, and extinguishes the rights and duties formerly vested in the parent or guardian, or in any other person by order of a court. The applicants must fully understand this.

Where an application is made by the mother or father of the child alone, the guardian *ad litem* must discuss the reason for the exclusion of the other natural parent, and where it is made by one only of a married couple, he must question why the other is not involved in the application. If the answer raises any doubts in his mind he should report to, and seek the advice of, the court.

In cases where the application is made by a married couple, although the method of interviewing is left to the discretion of the guardian *ad litem*, he is well advised to see the couple both individually and jointly. A couple seen together may well present a united front, declaring their motives to be mutual and expressing a joint desire to adopt a child. If either one is being influenced by the other this may well be camouflaged when they are seen together. Interviewed individually, they may show that the situation is quite different. The proposed adoptive father, for instance, may then make it clear that *his* desire to adopt is not quite as strong as his partner's but that he feels he must go along with her to avoid the possible collapse of their marriage. Information of this nature may not in itself be sufficient grounds for opposing the application, but it may lead to the disclosure of other factors which indicate that adoption could be a considerable risk for the child. Revelations of this nature are unlikely to be made when the couple are interviewed together.

Most adoption cases are pleasant from the start and move smoothly to a satisfactory conclusion, but this should never be taken for granted, and the guardian *ad litem* should never be afraid to make it clear that his interviews with the applicants must be of a very personal nature.

Some applicants do tend to resent the personal and intimate questions put to them, but most accept them readily. This is particularly so when it is pointed out to them that it is necessary to ensure that the child's interests are safeguarded, and that the applicants themselves would undoubtedly like to think that every precaution was taken to ensure a correct decision if it were their own child being placed for adoption.

Social workers (and probation officers) very often see adoption cases as the most pleasing and satisfying part of their work. They seldom carry the tensions and anxieties of so many other tasks in their profession. All this is true, but a warning note needs to be sounded. Because of the satisfaction adoption so often brings, it is very easy to become too friendly with the applicants. Without being too condemnatory over this, it should be recognised that in some instances it could be damaging and at best it is not professional. The practice should be avoided as it can lead to a decision being made before sufficient investigation is completed.

A friendly approach is vital; applicants are aware of all that is at stake, and may well be passing through a period of uncertainty, of joy mixed with concern that they may yet lose the child they are growing to love. They need therefore to be set at ease, so that they can talk freely of themselves, and of the events that are taking place in their lives, and this can only be achieved through a friendly approach. However, the guardian *ad litem* must temper this friendliness with the understanding that a person is being thoroughly investigated, and that he must satisfy the investigator that there is no impediment to his becoming an adoptive parent. The responsibility placed upon the guardian *ad litem* is far too great to permit intimacy.

In interviewing the applicants, he has a duty to find out the state of their marriage, and whether it has the stability likely to provide a sound basis for a secure parental relationship with an adopted child. If there is a relative residing in the household, it is essential to know as much as possible about him. This may lead to still more personal and intimate questions, but there must be some indication of how much the relative may be involved in the day-to-day care of the child, or other matters relating to the child's interests and future. It must be made clear whether the relative is a suitable person to have contact with the child, and particularly that he has not been prohibited from such contact as a result of specific conduct or offences relating to children. The same applies to a lodger or any other person from the age of sixteen who is residing in the household. Fortunately, such situations are rare, but every case must be treated with the same care and thoroughness.

The irrevocable character of an adoption order must be imprinted in the mind of the investigator, as it is in the mind of any applicant, or a mother who is relinquishing all her parental rights and duties in respect of the child. He must be conscious of the fact that his report and recommendation to the court are vital factors in the making of an adoption order, and that once this is made he has no opportunity of altering the situation.

It is not enough to enter the home of an applicant to have a quiet friendly chat about the application which has been made. It is essential that all particulars of the accommodation be seen and noted. The situation in the lounge (which has been prepared for a visit) may be quite different from that in the bedroom or other parts of the house; the whole residence should be inspected, and note taken of any significant feature which may be detrimental to the needs of the child. This may be discussed with the applicant.

If there are other children in the family, it is essential to know how old they are, whether they are natural children of the applicants or adopted, and whether the accommodation is sufficient for their needs. In any family, accommodation is very important; it can play a part in group or peer interactions – a factor which merits serious consideration. The standard of comfort is also worthy of note although this must be left to the good judgement of the guardian *ad litem*. Material factors must not be overlooked though they should take second place to emotional stability and security within the home. Consideration must also be given to garden space, play facilities within the home and in the area, and an effort should be made to look at the type of community of which the child will become a member.

In addition, it is the duty of the investigator to examine the means of the applicants, and where appropriate, the right to or interests in property (under disposition already made) which the child stands to gain if adopted.

Although in themselves the applicants may appear to be healthy, no child must be exposed to a health hazard, and therefore it should be ascertained whether the applicants suffer or have suffered from any serious illness, and whether there is any history of tuberculosis, epilepsy or mental illness in the family of either applicant.

Except in the case of an application for a provisional adoption order (made only in the High Court or County Court) the guardian *ad litem* must inform the court if it appears to him that one or both of the applicants may not be domiciled in a part of the United Kingdom, the Channel Islands or the Isle of Man. It is therefore necessary that the guardian *ad litem* satisfies himself of the applicant's place of domicile, as it may be that the court to which the application is made does not have jurisdiction to hear the proceedings or make an order. The place of the applicant's birth will undoubtedly appear in the application form, but it must be checked whether that is the place of domicile.

Further duties made clear in the Adoption Rules 1976 are that the guardian *ad litem* must ascertain and inform the applicants

(a)   whether the child has been baptised, and if so, the date and place of baptism,

(b)   what treatment the child has received with a view to immunising him against disease,

(c)   what, if any, rights to or interests in property the child stands to retain or lose if adopted, and

(d)   whether an insurance policy for payment on the death of the child for funeral expenses has been effected.

It is evident that to obtain such information, if it is available, the mother of the child or any other person who has had his care (or anyone else who may be able to assist) must be interviewed.

Interviews: the parent

Perhaps the saddest part of the guardian *ad litem*'s duty is interviewing a mother or other person who is relinquishing all parental rights and duties over the child. Many are very distressed in such interviews, particularly as they have previously made known their views to an adoption agency or other party when first parting with the child. At this point, they frequently prefer not to be reminded of the action they have taken, possibly because in some cases this was taken out of necessity rather than desire. A great deal of tact, patience and skill are required in handling this interview since it can be a reopening of wounds which were in the process of healing.

Until section 14 of the Children Act 1975 comes into operation, enabling an adoption agency to apply to the court for an order freeing a child for adoption, this process continues. It is usually seen as one of the late opportunities a mother has of withdrawing her agreement to adoption. This too should be handled carefully, because it must be made known that at this stage the prospects of a child being returned have diminished considerably, and the welfare of the child will be given first consideration by the court.

Apart from the possibility of agreement being withdrawn, the guardian *ad litem* must have the mother's assurance that she wishes the child to be adopted, that she is aware of the significance and permanency of adoption and that her agreement is freely given.

It is necessary to learn about the mother, her background, the child and the father if possible, and all this information must be drawn from her in such a way as to minimise further distress. She may have to be put at ease by reassurance that the child is being well cared for and that the order, if made, will secure his future in a happy and loving home. To do this honestly and with sincerity, the guardian *ad litem* should see the child, more than once if possible, before interviewing the mother. Indeed, as soon as possible after his appointment the guardian *ad litem* is expected to see the child and to ascertain whether he is able to understand the nature of an adoption order; if he is, the court should be informed immediately. The child's feelings and wishes in the matter should be taken into consideration by the court in the making of its final decision.

Interviews: the respondents

Every person who is a respondent in adoption proceedings, or appears to have taken part in the arrangements for the adoption of a child, must be interviewed by the guardian *ad litem* (or by an agent appointed by him for that purpose); if any respondent is under the age of majority the court must be informed of this fact.

Those who are respondents in adoption proceedings and who have to be interviewed in accordance with the Adoption Rules are as follows.

(a)   Every person, not being an applicant, whose agreement to the making of the adoption order is required under section 12 of the Children Act of 1975. This refers to every person who is a parent or guardian of the child.

(b)   Any Local Authority having the parental powers and duties of a parent or guardian of the child by virtue of section 24 (2) of the CYPA Act of 1969. Such a child is the subject of a care order.

(c)   Any Local Authority in whom the parental rights and duties with respect to the child are vested, whether jointly or not, by virtue of section 2 of the Children Act 1948. This applies to the Authority which has assumed parental rights over one or both parents, and includes the situation in which a Local Authority has already passed a resolution assuming parental rights and duties in respect of one parent and proceeds to pass a similar resolution in respect of the 'other parent' because the first parent was, or appeared likely to become a member of the 'other parent's' household.

(d)   Any person liable by virtue of any order or agreement to contribute towards the maintenance of the child. This would cover a putative father or step-parent who has accepted the child as a child of the family.

(e)   In the case of an application made after the coming into force of section 60 of the Children Act of 1975, any voluntary organisation in whom the parental rights and duties with respect to the child are vested, whether jointly or not, by virtue of that section. In a situation

of this nature, the Local Authority will resolve that parental rights be vested in the voluntary organisation, and where it is considered that the organisation should no longer have such rights the Authority can vest them in itself.

(f) The Local Authority to whom the applicant has given notice of intention to adopt under section 3 (2) of the Adoption Act of 1958. Should this Authority in the person of the Director of Social Services be appointed as guardian *ad litem*, it is evident that no interview would take place, since the Authority's knowledge of the child through the adoption welfare would be incorporated in the final report. If however, a probation officer were appointed as guardian *ad litem*, the Local Authority involved in the adoption welfare of the child would be requested to furnish a written report on the child, for inclusion in or with the guardian *ad litem*'s report to the court.

(g) Any Local Authority or adoption agency named in the application or in a form of agreement as having taken part in the arrangements for an adoption cannot be appointed guardian *ad litem* as it is then presumed to have a vested interest in the case. The same applies to an adoption agency, though in each instance they are respondents in the case and are under an obligation to furnish reports to an independent guardian *ad litem* for transmission to the court.

(h) Any Local Authority having the child in its care under any enactment. This includes a child in care under section 1 of the Children Act of 1948, and those committed to care under the various enactments, including those covered by the Guardianship and Matrimonial Acts.

(i) Any voluntary organisation having the care of a child as defined by section 88(b) of the Children Act of 1975. This applies to the organisation which is deemed to have actual custody of the child, but has transferred that custody to an individual (foster parent) who does not have legal custody of him.

(j) In a case where the applicant proposes to rely upon section 11 (1) (b) (ii) of the Children Act of 1975, the spouse of the applicant. This refers to an application made by one person who has attained the age of twenty-one and is married, but where the spouses have separated and are living apart, and the separation is likely to be permanent. The spouse who is not party to the application is made a respondent and must be interviewed by the guardian *ad litem*.

It is possible for the court to direct at any time that any other person (not being the child) or body of persons be made respondents to the application. In regard to this matter, there is a duty laid upon the guardian *ad litem* that if he learns of anyone who thinks he has a right to be heard by the court in adoption proceedings, and the claim appears to be justified, this must be reported to the court for appropriate action to be taken. Included in this may be an interested relative, a person claiming to be the father of the child even though he may not be his guardian or paying maintenance towards his upkeep, or any person who is or has been married to the mother or father of the child and who may have to be joined as a respondent.

Interviewing every respondent in adoption proceedings is not simply to ensure that all the necessary agreements are given freely and unconditionally, but also to build up a sound picture of the child and his background, and of the prospective adopters. This indicates to the skilled guardian *ad litem* the needs of the child and the type of family into which he might best fit, and whether he and the applicants are suitably matched to ensure a successful family relationship.

It is true that all this will have been undertaken by the adoption agency or Local Authority and it is often considered that the duplication is unnecessary. However, it should be recognised that the guardian *ad litem* is an independent person in relation to the proceedings, and his unbiased approach to the investigations helps to ensure that no mistake is made in the placement of the child. Under the 1975 Act (when it is fully implemented) the duties and responsibilities may undergo some change, particularly when section 14, which gives the court power to make an order freeing a child for adoption, becomes operative. There may then be no duty laid upon the guardian *ad litem* to interview the mother of the child.

The importance of the guardian ad litem

An important change has been made in the 1975 Act which means that it will not always be necessary to appoint guardians *ad litem* upon the hearing of an adoption application. Section 20 of the Act provides that rules will be prescribed when a guardian *ad litem* must be appointed, and it appears that it will be left to the discretion of the court whether or not an appointment is made in other cases.

It does seem a little strange that an Act which has placed considerable emphasis on independent representation in other proceedings, is cutting down on this principle in adoption hearings, even though it has been stated (and one has to admit not without some justification) that the guardian *ad litem* does not provide an effective safeguard. It is true, as the Houghton Report says, that the guardian *ad litem* invariably endorses the adoption application, but surely an endorsement is no bad thing in a matter of such vital importance.

There is also much truth in the view that the guardian *ad litem* may be no better qualified, and quite possibly worse qualified than the agency's worker, who has carried out all the investigations and made the placement in relation to the adoption. This, however, suggests a need for ensuring that the qualifications of the guardian should be of the highest standard, rather than that the appointment should be limited to certain cases. The qualifications now expected of guardians *ad litem* should go some way towards this end.

Irrespective of a guardian's appointment, the right to report direct to the court, which is now to be afforded to the adoption agency, is most satisfactory; having been involved in all aspects of the adoption up to the hearing, the agency should have a right to representation in the court.

It is not possible at this stage to assess to which cases the appointment of guardian *ad litem* will be prescribed by rules, and those to which the appointment will be made at the discretion of the court. In relation to the latter, however, one can anticipate that courts will differ in their use of discretionary powers; whether or not this will be for the good of adoption hearings only time can tell.

Sections 14 and 20 of the 1975 Act have still to be implemented, but they should be noted carefully as they may have considerable implications on the actual duties to be performed by the guardian *ad litem* when they are brought into effect.

Further duties

Further information which the guardian *ad litem* must gather is the date on which the mother ceased to have actual custody of the child and to whom the custody was transferred. Indeed, he must ascertain who has had actual custody of the child throughout his life, and for what period or periods. Although there is no legal obligation to interview a putative father unless he has legal custody, or has been maintaining the child, it is now necessary to learn whether the putative father is proposing to make application for custody, and to decide whether he would be likely to succeed in obtaining custody of the child. This situation may have been dealt with by the adoption agency or Local Authority, but it is incumbent upon the guardian *ad litem* to satisfy himself regarding the position, and interview the putative father in appropriate cases.

In a few situations it may be necessary to inform the applicants that the court may refuse to grant an adoption order, and instead may commit the child to the care of the Local Authority, or that in granting an adoption order it will include a direction that the child be under the supervision of a probation officer or social worker. When custodianship proceedings become operative it may then be necessary to point out that a custodianship order rather than an adoption order might be made.

It is evident from all the foregoing that the duties of a guardian *ad litem* and the responsibilities which stem from them are considerable. If the interests of the child are to be properly safeguarded, the investigation and the interviews must be painstakingly and skilfully undertaken. The Rules make it clear what has to be done; the manner in which this is accomplished rests with the guardian *ad litem*.

In the case of RE H (Minors), the Family Division strongly criticised a guardian *ad litem* report prepared by a probation officer for not supplying sufficient information. Brevity is not the first consideration in these reports as every item noted should be carefully investigated and clearly indicated in the report.

The appointment is made well in advance of a court hearing, to enable the appointee to see the applicants and child on a number of occasions so that he may note the developing relationship between them. Ample time is also given to follow up all the necessary interviews, and to prepare a report which gives the court a clear and concise picture of the situation and enables it to make a sound decision.

Some of the interviews can in fact be passed on to colleagues in other areas if the person to be interviewed lives outside the area in which the proceedings are to be heard.

Investigation does not begin and end with interviews. There must also be observation: a keen look at all that is going on in the home, including the response of the child to the prospective adopters and any other children. The look of a child as he responds to the words and actions of the 'parents' can reveal a great deal which should not be lost on the guardian *ad litem*.

There must be feeling: a testing of the atmosphere, whether or not it is warm and inviting, whether homely or the reverse; anything that will show if the child's emotional as well as physical needs are being met.

There must be assessment: a drawing together of the facts gathered from all sources, and the weighing up of all that is heard and seen, so that a carefully constructed estimation of the situation can be presented to the court.

A note should be made of the fact that a Juvenile Court has no jurisdiction to hear an application for a provisional order. Where application for such an order is made in the County Court, before it can be granted, the applicants must produce an affidavit signed by an approved person who knows the laws of the country of domicile, and this fact must be declared in the affidavit.

The guardian *ad litem* in care and related proceedings

The Local Authority Circular (75) 21 states:

> Section 64 (Children Act 1975) introduces new sections 32A and 32B of the Children and Young Persons Act 1969, designed to safeguard the interests of children involved in care and related proceedings in Juvenile Courts and in appeals to the Crown Court against decisions reached in the Juvenile Court. Section 32A provides that if in these proceedings there is, or appears to be, a conflict of interests between the parents and the child, the court may order that the parents shall not represent the child or otherwise act for him in the proceedings.
>
> Section 32B provides that, having made an order that the parents shall not represent the child, the court may then consider whether it is necessary to appoint a guardian *ad litem* to act for the child in the proceedings. In unopposed applications for the discharge of care or supervision orders there is a greater onus on the court to make an order that the parents shall not represent the child and to appoint a guardian *ad litem*. In these cases the court is required to take these steps unless satisfied that it is not necessary to do so to protect the child's interests. The power of the court to make an order under section 32A or to appoint a guardian *ad litem* under section 32B may be exercised by a single Justice before the proceedings.

Under the Magistrates' Courts (Children and Young Persons) (Amendment) Rules 1976, and Justices' Clerks Rules 1970 as amended, these powers may also be exercised by a Justices' Clerk.

Section 64(part) in respect of unopposed applications for the discharge or variation of care orders and supervision orders was implemented on 26 November 1976. The need for an independent voice to speak for the child in care proceedings was highlighted in paragraph 227 of the Maria Colwell report which states: 'Had the views of an independent social worker been available to the court it would have had the assistance of a second opinion which might or might not have endorsed the conclusions and recommendations contained in the social worker's report.' (See LAC (76) 20.)

Although the court's powers to appoint a guardian *ad litem* in unopposed applications does not affect the existing power to grant legal aid to a child in order that he may be legally represented in care proceedings, nevertheless all concerned people welcome this additional and complementary safeguard for the child.

The use of a specific case, however, to advance the objective must have its critics since it is always so easy to be wise after the event. There may be a hope, but there is no certainty, that the appointment of a guardian *ad litem*, particularly in unopposed applications, will avoid another case like that of Maria Colwell. It should not be too highly anticipated that such appointments will close the doors to a tragedy of this nature.

In fairness to Local Authorities and to social workers throughout the country, unopposed applications are dealt with day after day, and this is more often a token of success than otherwise. Tragedies such as poor Maria's are rare, but unfortunately they are also sensational and quickly catch the public eye and arouse the public's passions. Because of this, social workers in particular must be watchful, thoughtful and always painstaking in making judgements and assessments on those under their care.

The knowledge that a guardian *ad litem* may be appointed in particular cases, however, may increase the watchfulness of the social worker and this must have some advantage.

The purpose of the guardian ad litem

Although the functions of a guardian *ad litem* in care and related proceedings differ from those in adoption proceedings, there is one common purpose. Both are appointed as independent persons to safeguard the interests of the child. In adoption cases care must be taken that the child is placed with the right persons, and that as far as it is possible to discern, his future is secure in every aspect. In unopposed applications for the variation or discharge of care or supervision orders, the court must be assured that the time is right for such action to be taken.

Very frequently, before a Local Authority or parent makes an application for the variation or discharge of a care order, the child who is the subject of the order has been 'home on trial' for a reasonable period of time. Progress throughout the period has been considered as satisfactory, or the situation has been such that the care order is thought to be unnecessary and the application has been made. Does the court decide under such circumstances that there is no need for the appointment of a guardian *ad litem*? If so, what are the criteria used to arrive at this decision?

In fact, because of the huge workload in any Social Services Department (which is likely to increase rather than decrease) it may well be that the supervision of the child and the home has been minimal; the progress may not have been as good as it appeared. Indeed, there have been occasions when such an order has been revoked, only for the whole situation to collapse shortly afterwards, causing even greater damage to the child.

It is a subject of great debate, how a court, a single Justice or a Justices' Clerk decides which child should have a guardian *ad litem*; in this respect the so-called separate representation may not be quite as satisfactory as it would appear. While there is a choice in deciding whether or not a guardian *ad litem* is appointed, there will always be errors of judgement, to the detriment of some unfortunate child. As with adoption proceedings at the present time, surely it would be much better to appoint guardians *ad litem* in *all* care and related proceedings, at least for all children under school-leaving age. The appointment of the guardian is supposed to be made where it appears to the court that it is in the interests of the child to do so. Many will say that it is in the interests of *all* children to have an independent representative in care and related proceedings, and this indeed is the view of the author.

Duties: the investigator

The duties of the guardian *ad litem* are laid down in the Magistrates' Courts (Children and Young Persons) (Amendment) Rules 1976, with which both social worker and probation officer should be acquainted.

The first role of the guardian *ad litem* is as investigator. With a view to safeguarding the interests of the child before the court he shall, as far as it is reasonably practicable, investigate all the circumstances relevant to the proceedings and for that purpose shall interview such persons and inspect such records as he thinks appropriate.

LAC (76) 20 visualises this role as one in which he will be required to ascertain the wishes and feelings of the child concerning the application (taking into account his age and understanding) and ensure that those views are made known to the court. He must also interview the child's parents and guardian, other members of their household or other persons in whose charge or under whose supervision the child has been, including any officers of the Local Authority involved in the application.

This could undoubtedly be a time-consuming exercise, particularly in cases where the child has experienced a number of moves during the period he has been in the care of the Local Authority. It is assumed that the guardian *ad litem* could seek written reports, especially from other bodies or establishments where the child has resided. As many children are placed in establishments well outside their home area, it is also assumed that reports may be received from colleagues within these areas.

A third task is to seek access to the records of the Local Authority and any other body which has had the responsibility for the care of the child in so far as those records contain background information on the history of the child, including the contents of any reports which are to be produced in court.

Local Authorities and other professional bodies are never particularly anxious to have their records open to inspection, as they have a right regard for confidentiality. The guardian *ad litem* should therefore be a well-respected person whose integrity is beyond reproach and whose status in the field of child care is high. He must be able to establish good relationships with the officers of those Authorities and bodies he has to approach for information, and convince them of a mutual desire to further the interests of the child.

In a situation where the Authority is quite convinced that an application should be unopposed, and the investigator's examination of the evidence leads him to think otherwise, a tricky situation can be created. The view of one professional against another may have to be dealt with tactfully and with considerable understanding, but there should be no question of compromise or of being 'talked out of' a doubtful situation. Where there is doubt there is danger, and action should be taken in the interests of the child. The court should be left to decide whose evidence carries the most weight.

The investigator must also consider the grounds on which the application is made and the evidence which it is proposed should be adduced in support of the application. In connection with this, it has been queried what criteria the court might use to decide on the need for the appointment of a guardian *ad litem* for a child. In the case of Maria Colwell, the little girl was 'home on trial' for a very brief period before an application to revoke the order was made, and this turned out to be fatal. Perhaps the highlighting of this incident may encourage the courts to decide that where any child is 'home on trial' and an application is made for variation or discharge of an order within a limited period (say probably three months) a guardian *ad litem* should automatically be appointed.

There certainly was evidence to suggest that Maria spent too short a period at home before the court revoked the care order, and this is undoubtedly one factor the guardian *ad litem* may have to consider when considering the grounds for an application.

It has been said that the child 'was returned to her natural mother because of the supposed ever-present loving care in a natural parent.' The same writer declared 'It was assumed in Maria's case that the loving care offered by substitute parents – her foster parents – could not match the unique loving care of her mother. That view is fallacious.'[3]

In looking at the evidence which is to be given to support an application, the guardian *ad litem* must be on his guard against using blood ties as the main or sole reason for supporting the application. If the parents are making the application, he must be satisfied that this is in the interests of the child. The evidence in support of an application must be substantiated by facts and careful assessment of the situation, otherwise the guardian *ad litem* must oppose it on behalf of the child. If the child is with foster parents who appear to be able to fulfil all the needs of a child in a way that is beyond the capacity of the parents, then in the interests of the child he should oppose any application for a variation or discharge of an order.

Finally, the investigator must obtain any other reports on the child, his present circumstances and the arrangements proposed by either party for his future, including if necessary an independent report on the child's physical and mental health; in fact, any further information the guardian *ad litem* considers important.

Where the guardian *ad litem* considers that any independent medical report on the child is needed, he should arrange with the relevant Local Authority (which pays his expenses) for a medical report to be obtained and paid for under the 'Arrangements for Payment of Doctors for Collaborative Services'. Where the guardian *ad litem* is a probation officer he should obtain the medical report under similar arrangements (through the Local Authority which is the linked paying Local Authority for the Probation and After Care Committee by whom the guardian *ad litem* is employed). (LAC (76) 20.)

It can be seen from all this that the guardian *ad litem* has a wide range of investigations to undertake, and the manner in which this is accomplished will depend on his calibre, professional standing, knowledge of child care and his conscientious application to duty.

Duties: the assessor

In the light of his investigations, the guardian *ad litem* must next consider whether it is in the child's best interests that the application to which the proceedings relate should succeed. In other words, he now takes on the role of assessor. All the information he has gathered, including written reports, personal interviews and appropriate notes from records and files, etc., will be assembled together and a careful assessment made of the situation. He should then be in a position to decide for himself whether the application should succeed or whether there are grounds for opposing it.

In the light of that decision he must then decide how the case should be conducted on behalf of the child, and where appropriate, instruct a solicitor to represent the child.

Duties: the advocate

Where the child is not legally represented, the guardian *ad litem* will act as advocate, and conduct the case on behalf of the child, unless he otherwise requests.

The decision on how the case should be conducted is dependent upon the assessment, made after a study of all the necessary information and evidence. If it is decided that the application should succeed and there is no cause to oppose a variation or discharge of an order, the guardian *ad litem*, as advocate for the child, will report the result of his investigations to the court, placing no barriers in the way of the applicants.

If the guardian *ad litem* decides that the success of the application could be detrimental to the interests of the child, then it must be opposed, and in order to secure the best assistance for the child, he may instruct a solicitor to defend him. This will be arranged by asking the court to grant legal aid to the child.

Although it would appear that the guardian *ad litem* has the authority to conduct the case himself with the consent of a child who is not legally represented, it is assumed he will rarely do so except in situations where it is considered the application should be successful. There may be occasions, however, when he is involved in defending the child's interests, in which case he should acquaint himself fully with the role of advocate, so that he achieves some skill in the art of examination and cross-examination. In situations where he has instructed a solicitor to represent the child, he may well be cast in the role of chief witness, on the child's behalf, so he should study the demands of this role.

Duties: the reporter

Where the guardian *ad litem* thinks it would assist the court, he must make a report in writing to the court. Rule 20(1) (a) of the Magistrates' Courts (Children and Young Persons) Rules 1970 states:
'(1)   Where the court is satisfied that the applicant's case has been proved (a) the court shall take into consideration such information as to the relevant infant's general conduct, home surroundings, school record and medical history as may be necessary to deal with the case in his best interests and, in particular, shall take into consideration such information as aforesaid which is provided in pursuance of section 9 of the Act of 1969.' This in effect is a social enquiry report.

A typical case in which the guardian *ad litem* may think the court could be assisted by such a report would be where the applicant has applied for the discharge of a care order and this has been granted. The guardian *ad litem* may, however, have prepared a written report outlining the social background of the child, recommending that if the care order is discharged a supervision order should replace it, as there is a need for some continuing supervision of the situation. In this way the guardian *ad litem*, acting in the interests of the child, must also prepare reports.

Further duties

The guardian *ad litem* must also perform such other duties as the court shall direct. Situations may arise when the court requires specific information on particular matter, and it may direct the guardian *ad litem* to obtain this, or to carry out any other duty relevant to the application.

When the court has finally disposed of the case the guardian *ad litem* must consider whether it would be in the infant's best interests to appeal to the Crown Court, and if so, he must give notice of appeal on behalf of the child.

In any application in which the child is being represented either by a solicitor or guardian *ad litem*, the parents or guardian of the child have the right (apart from any other right they have to take part in the proceedings), both to meet any allegations made against them in the course of the proceedings by calling or giving evidence, and also to make representations to the court where the court has made an order under 32A of the Act of 1969. This right should be exercised after the evidence of the respondent and that of the applicant in rebuttal have been delivered, but before either the respondent or applicant makes his final address to the court.

It is imperative that the guardian *ad litem* knows something of the order and method in these proceedings, and this is laid down in the Magistrates' Courts (Children and Young Persons) Rules 1970, as amended by the Magistrates' Courts (Children and Young Persons) (Amendment) Rules 1976. Indeed, in both care and criminal proceedings in the Juvenile Court the Justices are governed by these rules, and a sound knowledge of them considerably simplifies the social worker's (and probation officer's) roles in that court. They are an important tool in the hands of all those involved in the court and no social worker should be without a copy of them.

9. The Probation Officer

The probation officer plays a variety of roles in court, some of which are similar or complementary to the roles played by the social worker. Others are usually enacted by the probation officer, though not all are outside the scope of the social worker, and these will engage our attention in this chapter.

Not all probation officers find pleasure in being called officers of the court, as they feel this identifies them too closely with the judiciary. Some think that to be so identified is a hindrance to the social work they are trying to establish with the offender. The fact that their duties mainly lie within and emanate from the court seems less important than the relationships they must develop with their clients. Nevertheless they must appreciate that (as is plainly stated in the Probation of Offenders Act 1965, as amended) they are generally linked to a court on their appointment. They are employed to serve the court, though their service extends beyond this sphere. Duties they have to perform, as set out in the Probation Rules, are:

(a) after care supervision of offenders following discharge from detention centre, Borstal and prison,
(b) investigating and reporting on matters relative to the custody, maintenance or education of a child,
(c) investigating and reporting on prescribed matrimonial causes,
(d) assisting or attending applications, with a possible view of effecting conciliation in matrimonial differences,
(e) acting as guardian *ad litem* in adoption proceedings, extended to care proceedings under the Children Act 1975,
(f) making enquiries in relation to applications to marry, and
(g) making application to the appropriate court for the amendment, discharge or variation of a probation order and dealing with a breach of probation through the court.

It can be said that whereas the Juvenile Court is very much the scene of the local authority worker, the Magistrates' Court and Domestic Court in particular are very much the domain of the probation officer. Each, however, has duties to perform in all courts. The nature of their employment demands a different approach to their task, though the methods employed to effect a satisfactory result may have very much in common. This is understandable as both are primarily social workers.

A general distinction which can be made between the two professions (although this is not clear cut), is as follows. The probation officer is essentially dealing with crime and the criminal, and this tends to place the emphasis of his work on the individual. The social worker, on the other hand, is concerned with the social and welfare needs of the family and the community, and is more likely to see the offender in relation to the family unit. With neither worker, however, is either the family or individual ignored.

The official purpose of a probation officer's duty is not attempting to rectify that which is wrong within the family (although the officer would not neglect this if it was affecting the offender), but to treat, advise or assist the offender to avoid further trouble with the law. Very frequently, when there are no family or other ties, the officer has only the offender to work with, and irrespective of the methods used, the individual is the principal subject.

One difference in the treatment given to offenders by the two professions lends some substance to the view expressed above. The probation officer tends to make more use of the 'control method', that is, office interviews with the offender in a one-to-one situation. The social worker places emphasis on the 'situational method', seeing the offender at home, frequently with his family or at his place of residence.

This is not to suggest that these methods are mutually exclusive; both workers will experiment with different forms of treatment which may benefit the offender. It may be fair to say, however, that by the very nature of his work the probation officer will be much more involved in the reformation of the offender, though still very much concerned with his welfare.

Domestic proceedings in the Magistrates' Court

In relation to the probation officer's roles under the Guardianship and Domestic Proceedings Acts, etc., some of these have been examined in Chapter 6, as they are also applicable to social workers. The same applies to the role of guardian *ad litem* which has also been dealt with. However, there are several other situations which demand the special services of the probation officer in the matter of domestic proceedings.

Applications

Some years ago it was common practice, especially in the London Magistrates' Courts, for the probation officer to assist applicants to make application for a summons relative to matrimonial proceedings. The primary aim of this was to weed out frivolous or futile applications before they were heard by the magistrates.

The procedure involved seeing an unrepresented applicant before the hearing of an application, and advising on whether or not there was any ground for taking out a summons against a spouse. This pre-enquiry frequently revealed that the prospective applicant was less concerned to take out a summons than to obtain help and support in a matrimonial or other problem. In appropriate cases the probation officer would offer casework support.

Possibly because applicants are now more often legally represented, the probation officer is less used by the courts in assisting with applications. However, applications can be made privately by a single Justice or stipendiary magistrate with the clerk of the court and the probation officer in attendance.

Reconciliation between estranged parties

In some of these applications, the probation officer may be requested to explore the possibility of reconciliation. This is an undertaking in which the skills of the officer should be fully utilised. Any effort he can make to avoid the breakdown of a marriage (in particular where children are involved), is undoubtedly important.

At the same time, simply to be able to say to the magistrate that the parties' differences have been 'patched up' is not necessarily a sign of success, nor necessarily even a token of progress. Exploring the possibilities of reconciliation does not mean coercing the parties into this position, and the officer must not approach the situation with that end in view. A coerced party is most likely to resent the intrusion into his private affairs, and while paying lip-service to reconciliation may in time well make the situation worse for his partner.

There is no simple guide-line to direct when a marriage should continue or when it should end, as what is tolerable to one union is quite intolerable in a second. The greater the knowledge an officer has of the divergent opinions and attitudes of the partners in a marriage, and what they expect from and are able to give to the union, the better equipped he is to cope with the practicality and possibility of reconciliation.

Whatever other skills he possesses, the officer should be a good listener and observer. What he hears and sees will help him to assess the situation and enable him to open up fresh possibilities to both parties. In this way, and if it is obvious that neither party desires the break-up of the marriage, it may be possible to lead them towards considering or attempting reconciliation. He must make it clear, however (and be clear in his own mind), that the final decision is theirs and theirs alone.

Where there are children involved, he must be alert to their reactions to the marital situation, and note how they are being affected by their parents' attitude and behaviour. This is most important, because if the parties are not reconciled and the matter is brought to court, whether or not a matrimonial order is made, the court is required to consider the welfare of the children. This could lead to the question of custody, possibly even committal to care, and the parents must be made aware of this fact.

In any situation where the probation officer, social worker or any other person has attempted to effect reconciliation between estranged parties, where a court has adjourned a hearing for this purpose, a statutory duty is placed upon the officer to present a written report to the court whether or not the attempt has been successful. No other information must be included in the report.[1]

Means enquiry report

Under section 60 of the Magistrates' Courts Act 1952, as amended by section 83 of the Domestic Proceedings and Magistrates' Courts Act 1978, a probation officer may be requested by the court to investigate the means of the parties in domestic proceedings

(a) in which an order may be made for payment of money by any person, and

(b) for the enforcement or variation of any such order.

A direction may be given by the court to the probation officer to report his findings on the means enquiry either in writing or by an oral statement in court. No report must be made, however, until the court has decided all the issues arising in the proceedings other than the actual amount to be paid by the order when it is finally made. This also applies in proceedings for an affiliation order.

Where the probation officer is requested to prepare a written report for the court, a copy of this must be given to each party or to their legal representatives. The court may then, at its discretion, decide to read the whole or part of the report in court. It may also request the probation officer to give evidence on his report, and must do so if this is requested by either party or their representatives. When such evidence is given by the probation officer, either party can then give or call evidence with respect to any matter referred to in the report or in the evidence given by the officer.

The specific purpose of this investigation is to ascertain the means of the parties with a view to assisting the court in determining the appropriate amount of an order. In making the enquiry the first factor to be borne in mind is that the issue has been settled; in other words, the court has decided that the husband has to pay maintenance to his wife and/or children, or the wife has to pay maintenance to her husband and/or children, or the putative father has to pay maintenance for his child. Where proceedings relate to a variation of the order, the court has decided that there has to be a variation whether by an increase or decrease of the payments. To decide on the actual amounts to be ordered, the court must have information on the income and expenditure of the parties and any matters relating to their means.

As so many money payment orders are made by the court without the request for a means enquiry, it is reasonably safe to assume that as a result of the evidence given by the parties considerable doubt has been raised in the minds of the Justices regarding the means or circumstances of either one of them.

Some enquiries may be relatively simple and straightforward, while others may be more difficult and complex, requiring considerable skill, tact and patience on the part of the officer endeavouring to complete a thorough investigation.

One or both parties may be reluctant to disclose all income or other monies, and may make an effort to persuade the officer that expenditure is greater than is actually the case. Though every effort should be made to verify all statements, it must be recognised that this may not always be possible. The officer should be prepared to meet with anger and resentment in some cases, as this type of enquiry touches what is often a very delicate area. In seeking the information required, however, the officer does have the authority of the court, and this should be exercised when necessary.

As the investigation is made in order to assist the court to decide on the amount of an order, it is clear that the search must be deeper than could be accomplished by the magistrates in simply asking the parties to give statements of their means. The officer should therefore tabulate and verify where possible the stated income and expenditure of the parties. Statements of income should correspond with wages slips, etc., or be verified with employers, and claims of expenditure matched with bills of account, HP payment cards, rent books and other positive evidence where this is possible.

Special factors relating to the parties' circumstances and needs should not be overlooked, as they may be important to the court in reaching a final decision. These factors will naturally differ from case to case and it is not possible to detail them here. As an example, however, a case was quoted in 2 ALL E.R.C.A. (1968), where the parties separated by mutual consent, the wife taking the child of the marriage with her: 'Maintaining the child might involve the wife in expenses over and above that of feeding and clothing it; she might, for example, have to live in more expensive accommodation than she would live in by herself, and looking after the child might severely curtail, if not wholly take away her capacity to work and so reduce her income, a situation more likely to arise in the case of a young or sickly child.'

This indicates that changed circumstances and needs may affect the final order, and the officer should be aware of this in undertaking a means enquiry.

Application for consent to marry

This application is made by a young person over the age of sixteen and under the age of eighteen, who under normal circumstances is not permitted to marry without the consent of parents or other specified sources, unless consent is dispensed with by the court, the Registrar General or the Master of Faculties.

The areas in which the Registrar General and the Master of Faculties are able to dispense with consent are mainly where those who should give such consent are absent, inaccessible or under some form of disability such as insanity. Where any person refuses consent, then only the court has the power of dispensation.

In dealing with such applications (which may be heard in the High Court, the County Court or the Magistrates' Court, but are dealt with mainly in the latter), the probation officer may be asked to investigate the circumstances and report back to the court.

The officer may also have to investigate whether there is any other person or authority who should give consent but has not been approached. He must, therefore, be aware of all those persons whose consent is necessary. The full list is to be found in the Second Schedule of the Marriage Act 1948 to which reference can be made. It is also essential for the officer to know that if the minor is a widow or widower then no consent is necessary, and if it is found on investigation that consent has been given, then this cannot be withdrawn at any time before the marriage.

The main feature of the investigation is likely to be an examination of the reasons for a parent's or guardian's refusal to give consent, and the vital question to be answered is whether or not this is being reasonably with-held. Some withhold consent simply on the grounds that one or both of the couple are too young, and it has to be made clear that this in itself is not sufficient and is unlikely to be accepted by the court. Alternatively, the refusal may be because one of the parties is too young and the age gap between the couple too great. This will require more attention, and possibly an assessment of the strengths and weaknesses of a possible union.

Further barriers which may be raised are differences in religion, colour, status, maturity, and much more that one or two interviews will uncover. Discussions with parents, etc., may not always be pleasant, and the officer will need to use his own skill and judgement in forming an opinion from the facts elicited. The facts are of vital importance to the court, but his opinion or recommendation should also be stated, except in situations where the court has specified certain factors to be investigated.

Although very interesting, this kind of investigation occupies only a very small portion of the probation officer's time, and some officers never have the opportunity of such involvement.

Reports in divorce proceedings

I am indebted to J. B. Chapman, Court Welfare Officer at the Royal Courts of Justice, London, for this section on the work of the probation officer in court.

It is open to High Court judges, County Court judges or Recorders to make a direction for a Welfare Officer's report on the children involved in divorce or wardship proceedings. This may be because there is a contest for custody between the parties to the proceedings, because there are difficulties over access, or because the judge is not satisfied that proper arrangements have been made for the future welfare of the children. Under the terms of the Matrimonial Causes Act 1973, he has to be satisfied of this before making a Decree Absolute. Welfare Officers are part of the pro-bation service in England and Wales and are attached both to the High Court and County Courts.

Once a direction has been made and a case allocated to a Welfare Officer, that officer has to get in touch with the parties and arrange to visit them at a time when the children involved can be seen and interviewed, as well as any other persons who are directly concerned with looking after the child-ren or who may have been cited as being willing to do so. Such persons may be grandparents, foster parents, aunts, uncles or other relatives.

This outline of visiting gives little idea of the complexity of many cases where there are numerous children in different homes and visits may have to be repeated. If a child is in care, either under a voluntary agreement or a care order, contact must be made with the Local Authority Social Services Department, with a view to obtaining a report or information concerning the child's history. In the majority of cases, contact must be made with the children's schools and progress reports obtained, while occasionally it may be necessary to obtain an interview with the Head Teacher. In other cases, where a child has a serious illness or disability, it may be necessary to contact a doctor or specialist and obtain a medical report. Where children are abroad, reports are requested from International Social Services.

Preparation of reports

When all the necessary information has been assembled, the Welfare Officer proceeds to write his report, which should include the following items.

(a) Particulars of the visits and contacts made in the course of the enquiry.

(b) A full and detailed description of the homes of each of the parties and any other house where the children may be living if they are not with either parent. This section should include a description of the neighbourhood and amenities, such as parks, recreation grounds, playgrounds, swimming pools, etc.

(c) An account of the parties concerned, their wishes, hopes, fears, and a profile of their personalities. In contested custody cases, the views expressed by the children themselves, if they are old enough, should be included. Judgement in this matter should be exercised by the officer.

(d) An assessment of the social contacts available to the children in each of the households concerned. Would the children be part of a warm, caring circle? Or would they be socially isolated and lonely?

(e) A consideration of the children's education, both present and future. If there is a choice of state schools or boarding schools, the officer should consider the advantages of each. He should also assess the reputation of the schools concerned, and obtain progress reports from the staff.

(f) Conclusions and in some cases, recommendations. Most High Court judges prefer to make inferences from the facts stated rather than to have definite recommendations. Most County Court judges expect recommendations. It is therefore necessary to bear in mind the type of court for which the report is needed.

Procedure before and in court

When the Welfare Officer's report has been completed and typed, it is filed in the Divorce Registry and copies are then available to interested parties on payment of a small fee. It follows that the counsel for both sides then examine the report very closely, to find out which parts are likely to benefit or prejudice their client's case.

At the court hearing, it is often desirable that the Welfare Officer should be present so that he may be questioned by the judge or by counsel on any aspect of his report, or on the accuracy of any of the particulars contained in it. It is essential to ensure total accuracy, and extreme care must be taken to avoid making references which may not stand up to examination and questioning.

Often the judge may conduct a dialogue with the Welfare Officer while the latter is in the witness box, asking his opinion about the advisability of pursuing certain courses, such as making a supervision order. This can be done under section 44 of the Matrimonial Causes Act 1973.

Procedure after the court hearing

Immediately after the hearing, there are usually matters over which the counsel will wish to consult the Welfare Officer. These often relate to access, which may have been closely defined by the judge. In certain cases, the judge may request that the Welfare Officer is present on the first occasion of access. In other cases, the details of access are left to the Welfare Officer to work out with the parties and their counsel. Sometimes the Welfare Officer may be required to inspect a home which was not ready or available on the date of the hearing. Welfare Officers may be required to keep in touch with the parties and the children pending a further hearing of the case, without any supervision order being made. An increasing number of cases of this kind are occurring.

To sum up, then, the task of the court Welfare Officer is to provide the court with the fullest possible background information about the parties, the children and other persons concerned. He must bring out all the facts which may help in the making of decisions about custody or access, or which may be needed in order to assess the existing situation.

Probation orders

Probation orders are applicable only to the probation service and form no part of a local authority social worker's duties within the court.

The order made in the Magistrates' Court is in some respects the equivalent of a supervision order made in the Juvenile Court, in that they both offer treatment in the open under the supervision of a social worker.

Section 2(1) of the Powers of the Criminal Courts Act 1973, makes it clear that a probation order is an alternative to a sentence, and as such does not count as a conviction.

The Sentence of the Court (HMSO 1978) explains the intentions of probation in these terms:

> The fundamental aim of probation, as of all methods of penal treatment, is to uphold the law and protect society. The particular object of placing an offender on probation is to leave him at liberty in the community but subject to certain conditions regarding his way of life, with skilled help available to him from the probation service to cope with the problems and difficulties that may have led to his offending, and with an obligation to co-operate with his supervising probation officer as regards reporting, receiving visits and heeding the advice given to him.
>
> Through the discipline of submission to supervision by a probation officer, this method of treatment seeks both to protect society and to strengthen the probationer's resources so that he becomes a more responsible person. . . .

The duty of the probation officer as defined officially is to advise, assist and befriend the probationer, and the main demands made on the probationer are that he lives an honest and industrious life, is of good behaviour and keeps in touch with the probation officer as and when required. This includes receiving visits from the officer at the probationer's normal place of residence.

Under the Criminal Law Act 1977, it is within the powers of the court to make an order for a minimum period of six months and a maximum period of three years, and the Secretary of State is empowered to vary by order both the minimum and maximum periods.

Additional requirements can be inserted in the order at the discretion of the court; these may cover such subjects as residence, medical treatment, attendance at a day centre and anything else which may ensure the good conduct of the offender and help him not to offend again.

Though there are differences of opinion on the matter, it is probably safe to assume that the order has a proven record of effectiveness with a wide range of offenders; however, careful assessment is vitally important in determining who might benefit from this form of treatment.

Discharge of probation orders

Probation orders are subject to discharge and amendment and it is possible for the probationer to be brought back to court to be dealt with for a breach of its conditions.

Very frequently two courts are involved with one probation order: the court making the order, which is the one before which the offender appeared in relation to an offence, and the supervising court, within whose area the offender resides. A probation order names the Petty Sessions area in which the offender resides, and requires that he be under the supervision of a probation officer appointed for or assigned to that area. These points are important in considering the discharge, amendment or breach of an order.

An application for the discharge or amendment to an order may be made by the probation officer or the probationer to the supervising court (which in some cases may also be the court which made the order). The exception to this is that where the court which convicted the probationer or heard his appeal is the Crown Court, then power of discharge lies with that court if a direction has been given that power be reserved to it.

If an application by the probation officer requests the substitution of a conditional discharge for the probation order, the former cannot extend beyond the normal date of expiry of the probation order. Such an application may be heard in the absence of the probationer with whom it should be discussed, but under such circumstances the probation officer must produce to the court a written statement by the probationer signifying that he understands the nature and effect of a conditional discharge.

Normally, the application for discharge is made when the progress of the probationer is satisfactory, or when it is considered the order has served its purpose. Note should be made of the fact that a probation order is automatically discharged if a probationer is sentenced for the offence for which he was placed on probation.

Amendments to probation orders

Amendments to a probation order cover quite a wide area and are made by the supervising court. Applications may be made by either the probation officer or the probationer to cancel or insert in the order any requirements made or which could be made by the court.

One application which may be made only by the probation officer is for the amendment of the order by substituting, for the Petty Sessions area named in the order, the Petty Sessions area where the probationer proposes to reside. This is undertaken when it is known that the probationer is moving from one area to another.

Difficulty can arise in this situation if the order contains requirements which cannot be carried out in another area, and the court cannot make the amendment unless these requirements can be cancelled or suitable requirements inserted to replace them. If the amendment is made, the original supervising court must send a copy of the order and other relevant information to the Justices' Clerk of the new area.

The other application which may be made only by the probation officer is for the variation or cancellation of requirement of medical treatment, where a medical practitioner decides

(a)   that the treatment of the patient should be continued beyond the specified period,

(b)   that treatment is required other than that which could be enforced through a probation order,

(c)   that the probationer is not susceptible to treatment,

(d)   that further treatment is not required, or

(e)   that he is unwilling to continue or direct treatment for the probationer.

A written report must be submitted by the practitioner to the probation officer who will then make the appropriate application to the court.

Any amendment requiring a probationer to reside in an approved probation hostel, home or other institution must be limited to a period not exceeding twelve months. No requirement can be made for treatment of a mental condition, unless the amendment is made within three months from the date of the original order. The court has no power to amend the order by reducing the probation period, or extending it beyond three years from the date it was first made.

Except in cases where the probationer makes the application himself, the supervising court will summons him to appear on the proposed amendment of an order, and no amendment can be made unless he expresses his willingness to comply with it.

Few amendments create problems for the probation officer as they are normally discussed with the probationer before an application is made.

Breach of probation

The right to return a probationer to court for failure to comply with the requirements of his probation order is the ultimate sanction the officer has in effecting the purpose of the order.

Few officers implement this right without giving careful and serious thought to the consequences it may have for the offender, being conscious of the fact that the court may deal either with the breach or with the original offence. Some are extremely reluctant to think in terms of a breach, possibly because to them it signifies failure to achieve anything with the probationer, or because it is thought that it will destroy a developing relationship, leaving little hope of future success. Neither is adequate reason for failure to carry out what may be a necessary duty.

The probation officer must never lose sight of the fact that probation is an alternative to a sentence, and the court has given the probationer an undertaking to carry out certain requirements, which were made known to him before the order was made. In making the order, the court placed responsibility on two persons: the probationer, to keep the requirements and thus avoid the possibility of being sentenced, and the probation officer, to ensure that the requirements were kept and to inform the court if they were not. Failure to carry out the requirements is a breach of promise by the probationer, and omitting to report the matter to the court is a breach of trust in the probation officer which should not be taken lightly.

It is not suggested that some misbehaviour on the part of the proba- tioner, or periods out of work, should be taken as a breach of the order. The requirement to be of good behaviour and live an industrious life suggests a continuing pattern of satisfactory conduct and industry, but not one which is free from deviation or lapse. An honest effort to meet the requirements is the expectation. The fact that a person is on probation indicates that there has been some departure from what is normally classed as good behaviour, and the need for outside supervision suggests that a measure of effort is needed from both the probation officer and the probationer to achieve satisfactory results. The purpose of the order and the requirements is to encourage and assist the probationer not to break the law again.

Should the probationer's behaviour be such, however, as to create a constant nuisance or danger to himself and others, then this must be seen as a breach of the order. The same applies to 'living an industrious life'. Where his conduct is affecting others, leading the probationer into dubious situations, or causing him to neglect or ignore the working situation, then this must be viewed in the light of a breach of the order.

Other breaches may be more clear cut, such as deliberately failing to report to the probation officer as and when requested, since this is in effect a refusal to accept supervision and a breach of the probationer's *voluntary* promise to the court.

Although some probation officers may be very reluctant to bring a probationer back to court, since he has not broken the law by committing another offence, nevertheless technically he has broken the law and brought the decision of the court into disrepute. If the officer fails to act on an obvious breach it could be said that he too is making a mockery of the court's decision.

There may be some value in noting that the law differentiates between a breach of probation and the commission of another offence during the period of probation, and the action the court can take in respect of either. The differences are contained in sections 6 and 8 of the Powers of Criminal

Courts Act 1973.

Section 6 deals with a breach of probation and the powers available to the appropriate court if the breach is proved or admitted. These are:

(a)   to impose a fine not exceeding £50,
(b)   to make a community service order in respect of the probationer,
(c)   to make an order for him to attend an attendance centre, or
(d)   to deal with the probationer for the original offence.

In laying information in respect of a breach, this can only be laid during the relevant period of the probation order and not after the period of the order has expired.

Section 8 relates to the commission of another offence during the period of the probation order and does not deal with the offence as a breach of the order nor give the court the same powers. The court can pass sentence on the further offence, and deal with the probationer on the original offence in respect of which the probation order was made. As distinct from section 6, however, an information can be laid after the expiry of the probation period if a further offence was committed within that period.

Some probation officers may feel strongly that a probationer should not be brought back to court unless he has committed another offence, but it is the duty of the officer to take action in respect of a deliberate breach of the order, otherwise the freedom granted by the court is turned into licence and the order ceases to have any value.

The courts having power to deal with a breach of probation, where the order was made by a Magistrates' Court, are

(a)   that court,
(b)   the supervising court,
(c)   the Crown Court.

Where the order was made by the Crown Court, they are

(a)   that court,
(b)   the supervising court in respect of the breach, but not for the original offence. If this court does not deal with the breach it can instead commit the probationer to the Crown Court.

The courts having power to deal with a probationer who has committed a further offence, where the order was made by a Magistrates' Court, are

(a)   that court,
(b)   the supervising court,
(c)   if he appears in another court on the further offence, that court with the consent of the court which made the order, or of the supervising court,
(d)   the Crown Court.

Where the order was made by the Crown Court, that is the relevant court for the further offence. If a Magistrates' Court convicts a probationer on a further offence, it may commit him to the Crown Court which made the order to be dealt with for the original offence.

The probation officer's procedure for dealing with a breach of probation and, where necessary, following the commission of a further offence by the probationer, is as laid down in the Powers of Criminal Courts Act 1973. He must lay an information before a Justice acting for the Petty Sessions area in which the court making the order or the supervising court acts. Should it be necessary to apply for a warrant (as when the offender cannot be found), then the information must be in writing and confirmed on oath before the Justice. The information will give brief details of the breach or other matter to be considered, and if he is satisfied with this the Justice or stipendiary magistrate will issue a summons or warrant requiring the probationer to appear at a specified court.

Although in most cases the probationer will admit the breach, there are occasions when this will be denied, and in such circumstances the probation officer must prepare his evidence carefully. His role will be that of prosecutor, and a study of this as it is outlined in Chapter 3 may be helpful.

There have been complaints that some probation officers are far too reluctant to take action on a breach of probation and that they place undue emphasis on the protection of their probationers. It may therefore be well to reiterate that probation is an alternative to a sentence, made at the discretion of the court to help the offender but carrying with it certain requirements. The offender has freely accepted the conditions, and must be prepared to accept the consequences if he breaks them. The probation officer is equally well aware of the position and has probably recommended the probation order. He too has a responsibility to ensure that the requirements of the order are fulfilled, and to be prepared to act if they are not.

10. The Conduct of the Social Worker in Court

As we have seen, the social worker and probation officer have a variety of roles to play within the court setting. In each case it is important to have a sound knowledge of the general situation, the expectations of the court and the function of that particular role.

The attitude of the social worker to his part in the court proceedings is of primary importance, and much of the mutual criticism of magistrates and social workers could be avoided if the right attitude were adopted on all sides.

A meeting point between the social worker and the magistrate is mutual respect; respect for each other as individuals and for the duty each performs. This has to be earned, and certainly cannot be achieved by conduct on either side which is only calculated to generate enmity. Both must endeavour to break down any barriers in their combined efforts to arrive at the right decision and adopt the best course of action.

The social worker must respect the fact that magistrates are not social-work orientated, nor, under the present legal constitution, are they intended to be. They should be prepared, however (and they often are), to accept social work assessments, where these seem to be in keeping with the facts presented.

The magistrates must respect the efforts made by a social worker (for instance, in compiling a social enquiry report), and appreciate that the worker does see a multiplicity of factors affecting the client, his reactions and his probable needs, leading the worker to make an educated recommendation.

This does not mean, of course, that the recommendation must automatically be accepted, since other expert information may also be available. The decision ultimately lies with the magistrate, and this fact must be accepted with respect.

Our modern system, with its successful combination of Justices and probation officers, took some time to achieve, and developed mainly as the Justices became aware of the excellent work performed by the probation service. The close communication which grew between them, and the evident success of the system, led to the courts placing great confidence in the recommendations of the probation officer.

In divorce proceedings, as we have seen, the judge often conducts a dialogue with the Welfare Officer while the latter is in the witness box, asking his opinion on the various possible courses of action. This kind of communication undoubtedly reveals the mutual respect which is so vital in all court transactions.

The Children and Young Persons Act 1969 certainly offers opportunities for discussion and consultation between the magistrates and the social services, and recent joint reports from the Association of Directors of Social Services and the Magistrates' Association are steps in the right direction. Although there are disagreements on certain issues, nevertheless this co-operation must eventually benefit the offender. However, one would like to see more communication between individual social workers and the Justices, as it is the former who are in the front line of the service and they do need to establish a direct link with the courts.

There is no obvious solution to many of the problems confronting the social worker and the Justices today, but disrespect, complaints and criticism can only worsen the situation. There is without doubt a great need for mutual respect, communication and co-operation in all court matters if any measure of success is to be achieved.

Notes

Chapter 1 The Social Worker Has a Part to Play

1. Domestic Proceedings and Magistrates' Courts Act 1978, s. 80 (2), amending Magistrates' Courts Act 1952, s. 56 A (2).
2. J. D. McLean, *The Legal Context of Social Work* (Butterworth, 1975).

Chapter 2 The Magistrate and the Clerk

1. See Frank Milton, *The English Magistracy* (Butterworth, 1967).
2. Children and Young Persons Act 1933, s. 45. Interpretation Act 1889, s. 13 (11).
3. Juvenile Court Rules 1954, as amended.
4. CYPA 1933, Schedule 2 (2) (c).
5. ibid. Schedule 2 (2).
6. ibid. s. 47 (2).
7. ibid. s. 49 as amended by CYPA 1963, s. 57, and CYPA 1969 s. 10 and Schedule 5.
8. CYPA 1933, Schedule 2 (2) (c).
9. Magistrates' Courts (CYP) Rules 1970, Part 2.
10. ibid. r. 13 (2).
11. Magistrates' Courts Act 1952, ss 57 (2) and 58 (1), as amended by Domestic Proceedings and Magistrates' Courts Act 1978, as 81 (1) and 82.

Chapter 3 The Prosecutor and Advocate for the Defence

1. See Richard Bruce, *Success in Law* (John Murray, 1978).
2. See C. C. H. Moriarty, *Police Law* (22nd ed., Butterworth, 1970) p. 97 for valuable information on evidence.
3. ibid.

Chapter 5 The Social Worker as Applicant, Witness and Advocate

1. Children and Young Persons Act 1969, s. 28.
2. Children and Young Persons Act 1933, s. 107 (1).
3. Children and Young Persons Act 1969, s. 2 (10) 20 (1).

Chapter 6 The Social Worker as Reporter

1. See Martin Davies and Andrea Knopf, *Social Enquiry Reports and the Probation Service* (HMSO, 1973), Peter Ford, *Advising Sentencers* (Blackwell, 1972), and also F. G. Perry, *A Guide to the Preparation of Social Enquiry Reports* (Barry Rose, 1975) — a good practice booklet.
2. Section 34 (3).
3. For the sake of convenience the term *child* is used throughout this chapter to indicate both a child from birth to thirteen years, and also a young person of fourteen to sixteen years inclusive.
4. Useful reading for this purpose includes: *The Sentence of the Court* (HMSO, 1978); J. Watson and P. M. Austin, *The Modern Juvenile Court* (Shaw, 1975); H. K. Bevan, *The Law Relating to Children* (Butterworth, 1973); and Brian Harris, *The Criminal Jurisdiction of Magistrates* (Barry Rose, 1977).
5. Brian Harris, *The Criminal Jurisdiction of Magistrates* (Barry Rose, 1977).

Chapter 8 The Role of Guardian *ad litem*

1. As the representative of a Local Authority, the Director of Social Services is normally appointed by the court as guardian *ad litem*, but the duties of the appointment are undertaken by one of his social workers. Here the term is used to refer to the social worker and not the Director.
2. In adoption proceedings the guardian *ad litem* may not be a member of the placing agency. If the Local Authority is the placing agency, the court must appoint a probation officer or an officer from another Authority as guardian *ad litem*.
3. See John G. Howells, *Remember Maria* (Butterworth, 1974).

Chapter 9 The Probation Officer

1. Domestic Proceedings and Magistrates' Courts Act 1978, s. 26 (2).

Index

96 *The Social Worker and the Courts*

Children Act 1948, resolutions under section 2, 16-17, 29-30
clerk, *see* justices' clerk
Colwell, Maria (case of), 69-70
committal:
  to care, *see* courts (orders); custodianship
  to Crown Court, 8, 89-90
County Courts, *see* courts
courts:
  aspects in general:
    civil procedure, 15-19
    conduct of social worker in, 91-2
    conflicts with aims of, 2-3
    defence, role of, 14-15
    prosecutor's role, 11-13
    resolutions under s.2 of Children Act 1948, 16-17, 29-30
    witness, qualities of a good, 13-14
  chairmanship of bench, 6-7, 8
  civil proceedings in, 8-9
  County:
    marriage consent, 81-2
    see also adoption; custodianship; guardianship
  criminal proceedings:
    defence role, 14-15
    prosecutor's role, 11-13
  Crown:
    committal to, 8, 89-90
    powers as to probation, 89-90
  Domestic:
    adoption proceedings (for full details *see* adoption), 17
    applications before, 78
    conciliation attempts, 78-9
    custodianship proceedings, 19, 52-7
    divorce matters, 82-4
    marriage, consent to, 81-2
    matrimonial proceedings, 18, 52-7
    means enquiries, 79-81
    probation orders, 85-9
      breach of, 87-90
      discharge of order, 85-6
      purpose and use of, 84-5
      variations of, 86-7
    probationary work and, 77-82
    scope of work of, 1, 9
    see also adoption; custodianship; guardianship
  High:

marriage consent, 81-2
  see also adoption, custodianship; guardianship
  jurisdiction of, 7-9
  Juvenile:
    and Domestic Court contrasted, 76
    jurisdiction, 6
    restrictions on disclosing identity, 6
    size, etc. of bench, 6
    social enquiry reports for, 36-8
    woman must serve on bench of, 6
  Magistrates, 5-10
    powers as to probation, 89
    social enquiry reports for, 45-7
  orders of:
    care, 28, 49
    custodianship, 53-5
    interim, 29
    maintenance, 79-81
    matrimonial, 50-52
    place of safety, 26
    probation, *see above* in this entry *under* domestic
    supervision, 67-8, 84-5
    stipendiaries, 6, 7
    see also adoption; care proceedings; custodianship; guardianship; matrimonial
Crown Court, *see* courts
custodianship, 1
  application for order of, 54-5
  court order for, explained, 54-5
  proceedings, 19
  reports in, 53, 55-7
  see also courts; guardianship

decree absolute, 82
defence, court role, duties and rights of, 14-15
Detention Centres, 76
divorce matters, 82-4
Domestic Courts, *see* courts

enquiry reports, *see* reporting
evidence:
  examination of witnesses, 12-14
  hearsay, 12

fostering, *see* custodianship proceedings; guardianship

guardianship, 1
  ad litem, 17

as to adoption, 59-69
  interviews (with applicants),
    60-63, (with parents), 63-4,
    (with respondents), 64-6,
  significance of appointment
    as, 66-7
  probation officer as, 76
County Court cases, 59, 62
DHSS circular on, 58
High Court cases, 59, 62
investigative duties in care, etc.
  proceedings, 71-5
local authority ineligible as, 59
of minors in general, 48-9
proceedings for, 18-19
purpose of in care, etc. proceedings, 70-71
role of, 58-75
  importance of, 66-7
  specific duties of, 67-8
  special duties in care etc. pro-
    ceedings, 69-75
  see also adoption; care proceed-
    ings; custodianship; probation
    service

hearsay, 12
High Court, *see* courts

Interim Orders, 29
interviewing, 41-2
in adoption cases:
  applicants, 61-3
  parents, 63-4
  respondents, 64-6

justices, *see* magistrates
justices' clerk, role of, 9-10
Juvenile Bureaux, 23-4
Juvenile Courts, *see* courts

Legal Context of Social Work
  (McLean), 2
legislation, *see* Acts of Parliament;
  Rules and Regulations
Local Authorities:
  as *in loco parentis*, 25
  cannot refuse a care order, 49
  circulars of, in care etc. pro-
    ceedings, 69-75
  court actions by, 27-9
  has no right of representation
    under Family Law Reform Act
    1969, 53
  power to assume parental rights,
    16-17

power to bring care proceedings; 15
powers under Children Act 1975,
  20-21
social worker representative of,
  25
supervision, 67-8
see also adoption; care proceedings; child; courts; custodianship; guardianship; reporting;
  social worker

magistrates:
  role of, 5-9
  see also courts
Magistrates' Courts, *see* courts
marriage, applications for consent
  to, 81-2
matrimonial proceedings, 1, 18, 50-
  52, 53
  see also custodianship; probation
    service
means enquiry reports, 79-81
minors, application for consent to
  marry, 81

NSPCC, power to bring care proceedings, 15

orders of court, *see* court

parents:
  and Place of Safety Orders, 26
  and the social enquiry report,
    40-42
  custody decisions and, 18-19
  interviews with, in adoption
    cases, 63-4
  local authority can assume rights
    of, 16-17
  may not seek custodianship
    order, 54
  putative fathers, 67-8, 80
  significance of social enquiry
    reports, 37, 55-7
Place of Safety Orders, 26
police:
  power to bring care proceed-
    ings, 15-16
  role and duties of, 20-24
prison, after care following, 76
Probation Orders, *see* courts (Domestic)
probation service:
  contrasted with social worker,